Civic Capitalism

Civic Capitalism

Colin Hay and
Anthony Payne

polity

Parts I and III copyright © Colin Hay and Anthony Payne 2015
Part II copyright © Polity Press 2015

The right of Colin Hay and Anthony Payne to be identified as Authors of this
Work has been asserted in accordance with the UK Copyright, Designs and
Patents Act 1988.

First published in 2015 by Polity Press

Polity Press
65 Bridge Street
Cambridge CB2 1UR, UK

Polity Press
350 Main Street
Malden, MA 02148, USA

ISBN-13: 978-0-7456-9206-7
ISBN-13: 978-0-7456-9207-4(pb)

A catalogue record for this book is available from the British Library.

Typeset in 11 on 13 pt Sabon
by Toppan Best-set Premedia Limited
Printed and bound in Great Britain by CPI Group (UK) Ltd, Croydon,
CRO 4YY

The publisher has used its best endeavours to ensure that the URLs for external
websites referred to in this book are correct and active at the time of going to
press. However, the publisher has no responsibility for the websites and can make
no guarantee that a site will remain live or that the content is or will remain
appropriate.

Every effort has been made to trace all copyright holders, but if any have been
inadvertently overlooked the publisher will be pleased to include any necessary
credits in any subsequent reprint or edition.

For further information on Polity, visit our website: politybooks.com

Contents

Contributors

Colin Hay is Professor of Political Science at Sciences Po, Paris, and Affiliate Professor of Political Analysis and Co-Director of the Sheffield Political Economy Research Institute (SPERI) at the University of Sheffield. He is the author of many books including *The Failure of Anglo-liberal Capitalism*, *The Political Economy of European Welfare Capitalism* (with Daniel Wincott) and *Why We Hate Politics*.

Anthony Payne is Professor of Politics and Co-Director of the Sheffield Political Economy Research Institute (SPERI) at the University of Sheffield. He is the author and editor of many books including *The Global Politics of Unequal Development*, *Development* (with Nicola Phillips) and *The Handbook of the International Political Economy of Governance* (with Nicola Phillips).

Fred Block is Professor of Sociology at the University of California, Davis. His most recent book is *The Power of Market Fundamentalism: Karl Polanyi's Critique* (with Margaret R. Somers).

Colin Crouch is Emeritus Professor of Governance and Public Management at the University of Warwick Business School. His most recent book is *Making Capitalism Fit for Society*.

Andrew Gamble is Professor of Politics at the University of Cambridge and a Fellow of Queen's College. His most recent book is *Crisis without End? The Unravelling of Western Prosperity.*

Ian Gough is Visiting Professor at the Centre for the Analysis of Social Exclusion at the London School of Economics and Professor Emeritus at the University of Bath. His recent work has focused on climate change and sustainable welfare.

Gavin Kelly is Chief Executive of the Resolution Foundation think-tank and **Conor D'Arcy** is a Policy Analyst at the Resolution Foundation.

Ruth Levitas is Emeritus Professor of Sociology at the University of Bristol. Her most recent book is *Utopia as Method: The Imaginary Reconstitution of Society.*

Mick Moran is Emeritus Professor of Government at the Manchester Business School. His most recent book is *After the Great Complacence: Financial Crisis and the Politics of Reform* (with Ewald Engelen, Ismail Ertürk, Julie Froud, Sukhdev Johal, Adam Leaver, Adriana Nilsson and Karel Williams).

Ann Pettifor is Director of Policy Research in Macroeconomics (PRIME) and a Fellow of the New Economics Foundation. Her most recent book is *Just Money: How Society Can Break the Despotic Power of Finance.*

Matthew Watson is Professor of Political Economy at the University of Warwick. His most recent book is *Uneconomic Economics and the Crisis of the Model World.*

Preface

This little book is a book of its times in at least one un-equivocal and technical sense. It emanated from a series of blog posts that we wrote for *SPERI comment: the political economy blog* between November 2013 and March 2014. These posts were then gathered up into a SPERI paper published in May 2014. We are pleased to say that in both formats they attracted some attention from readers and we were emboldened to seek to develop the ideas further in this volume. We were also only too aware of course that, for the first time in our lives, we knew in advance the precise date of the next British General Election.

We would therefore like to thank a series of people who helped us get this book to press in quick time: John Thompson of Polity Press who took an immediate decision that this was a proposal worth endorsing; the 'commentators' on our original essay who responded willingly and quickly to our requests to see if they could help us take forward the debate about a potential civic capitalism; and Sarah Boswell and Laure Astill, successively the administrators of the Sheffield Political Economy Research Institute (SPERI), which we are proud to co-direct.

For us, SPERI has been great fun to set up and lead. We hope that this book not only serves well as a kind of 'manifesto' for its approach and work, but also says something of interest, and perhaps of importance, to the plight of Britain (especially) but other countries too as we all seek to build something better out of the global crisis of the last few years.

Colin Hay and Anthony Payne
September 2014

Part I

Civilizing Capitalism

Civic Capitalism

Colin Hay and Anthony Payne

As we struggle with the legacy of the crisis in which we are still mired and with the prospect of accelerating environmental degradation, it is time to ask not what we can do for capitalism but what capitalism can do for us, as citizens of a democratic society. In this short book, we seek to build on the analysis of the enduring crisis of what we will term the 'Anglo-liberal growth model' to set out a coherent account of the steps required to build an alternative that is more sustainable socially, economically and environmentally.

We argue that it is time to move on from the Anglo-liberal model of capitalism whose failings were so cruelly exposed by the crisis. In the process, we outline a new model that will work better in advanced capitalist societies, showing how this might be achieved in Britain today. This we term *civic capitalism* – the governance of the market, by the state, in the name of the people, to deliver collective public goods, equity and social justice. Its core and defining ethos reverses the long ascendant logic of Anglo-liberalism in which citizens have been made to answer to the perceived logics of the capitalism they have been required to serve. That reversal, we argue, is not only intensely desirable; it is also absolutely necessary.

The crisis shows us that we can no longer be driven by the perceived imperatives of the old model and by those who have claimed for far too long – as it turns out, quite falsely – to be able to discern for us the imperatives of the market. It is now time to ask what capitalism can do for us and not what we can do for capitalism.

Getting What Went Wrong Right

Crises, almost inevitably, prompt recriminations – the present crisis more than most, in part because of its severity, in part because of the context of pervasive political disaffection and distrust in which it has been played out. But, if we are genuinely to learn the lessons of the crisis, it is time to put recriminations behind us. And, if we are not just to learn from those lessons but actually to put that learning into practice, we must also move on from the mawkish (if necessary) analysis of the failings of the Anglo-liberal model of capitalism which took us to the edge of the precipice in the first place. The moment has come when we need to start to pin some colours to the proverbial mast, outlining a new model that will work better where the old model failed. This is a bold endeavour, fraught with difficulties, both intellectual and political. But, if we do not try to tackle it, we shall have no excuse if we look back in a decade's time and find that a reconstituted bastard version of the old model is still intact – and that the systemic weaknesses which the crisis exposed remain unresolved and threaten us still.

But what do we mean in this context by a *model* of capitalism? Nothing more, but also nothing less, than a coherent framework of societal and economic goals and priorities and a supporting set of complementary institutions that both reflect and give rise to a coherent and distinctive way of conducting the daily business of a capitalist economy such as our own. Thus understood, a model should possess a clear sense of the vision of the good society to which it aspires. In that sense, it will be a model of development as much as a model of growth, and it needs to reflect and build from a consistent and defensible conception of social justice. Lastly, such a model should be applicable to a range of advanced post-industrial economies – not just to Britain alone – as well as offering insight into the many problems which capitalist economies face together and for which coordinated collective action is required. Indeed, if specified at a national level, such a model needs to be compatible with such collective and transnational strategies of coordination.

It is important also to emphasize what a model of capitalism is *not* – what it does not and cannot do. Getting our model of capitalism right will not and cannot tell us exactly what policies to follow in detail in every, or indeed any, given situation. Thus, whilst it might well insist both on the need to consider in a broad and inclusive way the wider societal and environmental consequences (or externalities) of economic policy choices and on the need to hold such choices to account in terms of societal notions of civic justice, it is most unlikely to tell us whether interest rates should rise or fall at a given point or at what level to set the aggregate burden of taxation. Similarly, it might suggest that a workable industrial policy is needed, but it will not indicate precisely which winners to back or even if backing winners is the best approach.

In other words, the task of setting out a new model of capitalism is more like designing a new car than offering advice to the driver from the passenger seat – and arguably there has been rather a lot of that already. It is also, critically, about offering a plausible narrative that explains to the citizens of our model capitalism what they are part of, how they might fit in, what gives their productive lives some meaning (and how the meaning it already has might be better supported and sustained). Capitalism needs to be seen to have a moral purpose and we need to be as clear about that moral purpose as we can be; otherwise, as we have seen in recent years, it is in danger of degenerating into an ugly and brutal rat race in which social and economic outcomes bear no relationship to considerations of social and economic justice. We need to restore that link and to take responsibility for it – in short, to re-moralize capitalism. That may sound naively idealistic. But our argument is in fact that such a capitalism is likely to be more sustainable, socially, economically and environmentally, than the amoral capitalism we have endured for so long.

Where, then, to begin? Political economy as a field has previously engaged extensively in discussion of 'models of capitalism' and 'models of development'. There is a vast literature out there (Albert 1993; Coates 2000; Crouch 2005; Hall and Soskice 2001; Schmidt 2002; Seldon 1990). But the truth is that it has rather run out of steam in the last few years and remains limited to the exposition of a small number of quite crude 'ideal types' (some of whose exemplars have revealed themselves to be far from 'ideal' when seen in the context of the crisis). The analysis has also tended to be static and has not coped well with the new realities of regional and global economic interdependence (Hay and Wincott 2012). Partly as a consequence (and, dominated, as it was, by equilibrium assumptions) it failed, quite profoundly and quite spectacularly, to see the crisis coming. As such, the existing literature does not provide a very useful starting point. Since it offered little insight into the pathologies of the old model, it is not well placed to lead us out of the crisis.

What we need instead, then, is to build an analysis of the old model from those more acutely aware, even during the benign tranquillity of the 'great moderation', of its inherent contradictions. We start with the nature of the old (Anglo-liberal) model itself. It has unquestionably failed us; but it is from that wreckage that we now need to build an alternative. In a previous publication (Hay 2013), one of us identified the following as the key features of this Anglo-liberal model:

- the hegemony of an assertive neoliberal ideology;
- an elite policy community increasingly trapped in its thinking within this narrow ideological framework;
- the wholesale deregulation of markets and the privatization of financial management;

- a high and increasing dependence on the supply of cheap hydrocarbons, with seriously damaging environmental consequences;
- the systemic accumulation of debt and the increasingly pathological dependence of consumption (and, in turn, growth) on such debt;
- an accumulation of risk within the economic system, with growth over time increasingly associated with accelerating exposure to that risk;
- the absence of a coherent theory of society, or social well-being, beyond the sum of individual, supposedly rational, goal-seeking;
- the consequent embedding of inequalities between and within countries; and
- a limited view of global governance as requiring little more than rules to manage competition between national economies.

A sensible and realistic next step in moving away from this model might therefore begin by simply adjusting, and of course in some cases redressing completely, each of these nine features. What sort of a model might then emerge? If we follow through the logic of the thought experiment we have just proposed, we proceed quickly to the broad outline of a new model of capitalism, characterized now by these rather different distinguishing features:

- the emergence of a more consciously held, open-ended and dynamic ideology that puts markets at the service of the public as citizens;
- a more interventionist role for the state animated by a sense of its civic duty;
- the coordinated re-regulation of markets and risk management, both as a collective public good and an antidote to unstable growth;
- the need for sustainability and serious engagement with alternative models of energy use and resource conservation;
- the promotion of sustainable development built upon investment, rather than debt-fuelled consumption;

- the development of an alternative currency of economic success (both domestically and globally), taking us beyond the crude measurement and slavish pursuit of economic output alone;
- the integration into this alternative model of development of a genuine social dimension that opens up different and more civic social policies and partnerships;
- a shared commitment to reducing prevailing levels of inequality between countries and peoples; and
- the creation of more intensive and sophisticated, flexible and deliberative, mechanisms of global governance capable of serving, and in part also reflecting, the guiding intelligence of the global economy.

In the sections which follow, we explore further and in turn each of these potential characteristics of a new model of capitalism. We see such a model as being appropriate to Britain and other advanced post-industrial economies, though we concentrate here on the implications of our account for Britain specifically. In the process, we seek to piece together a picture of this new model frame by frame in a cumulative and, we hope, coherent fashion. At each stage, we seek to relate the broader analysis and account to the particular choices that Britain faces today at this critical juncture in terms of its future social and economic development.

A final initial question arises, however, even at this early stage: namely, what to call this new model? After all, labels matter. A new model has to be readily accessible, engaging, broad-based and capable of delivering palpable improvement in the quality of life and work for the vast majority of citizens – particularly, perhaps, those who have been so egregiously let down by the old model. But it needs to be more than just 'populist' in orientation, given that so much more is at stake here than the provision of more 'bread' and better 'circuses'. In short, the new model of capitalism we need has to be productive and sustainable, as well as popular.

We think our model is best described as civic capitalism. Here we deploy the word 'civic' in its simplest and most straightforward sense – 'pertaining to' and 'working for' all of us in society, not just as consumers, or rational egotists, or even voters, but rather as *citizens* of a democratic polity. In the process of calling for and articulating such an alternative, we need to remind ourselves that capitalism can and must be made to work for us. We can no longer be driven by its perceived imperatives and by those who purport to be able to discern for us its needs. *It is time to ask what capitalism can do for us and not what we can do for capitalism.* If civic capitalism has a single mantra, then that is it.

Moving on from Old Ideological Certainties

Ideology, these days, is a dirty word – rarely if ever a term of self-description and invariably only ever something others have. Partly as a consequence, many like to think that in the pre-crisis world we were not governed by ideological thinking and that, having spent so long weaning ourselves off it in favour of technically proficient economic competence, the last thing that we need now is to rediscover its merits. Both claims are wrong.

For the crisis, we argue, is as much a product of an unacknowledged ideology as anything else. Indeed, it was only in the context of such an ideology that the laissez-faire policies of market liberalization favoured in the Anglo-liberal world could be seen as the very condition of good economic management. It is the crisis that reveals this as an illusion; and it is the crisis, and the lessons we draw from it, that requires us never to so mislead ourselves again. What this entails is not, however, 'the end of ideology', but rather the move from an unacknowledged, closed and static ideology to a more consciously held, open-ended and dynamic ideology – and, above all else, to one that puts the market in the service of the public, as citizens, rather than the citizens in the service of the market.

So what was the nature of the ideology that led us astray and how might the placing of citizens above the market and of civic values above market values start to put things right? There are many things to say here. First, the dominant ideology in the pre-crisis era was largely technical in character – whether manifest in the investment algorithms of financial market actors or the benign mood music generated by the credit-rating agencies or the light-touch regulatory dispositions of the institutions of depoliticized economic governance (Blyth 2013). It was this pervasive 'technicism' that made it more difficult to discern, less visible for what it was and all the more impregnable to contestation. Its formalism masked and hid from view its dubious economic premises and the benighted moral and political philosophy on which these typically rested (for an eloquent debunking of these premises, see Watson 2014).

Second, and more obviously, this background or *sotto voce* ideology was profoundly market-conforming in both its moral conviction as to the supremacy of purely market-based systems of allocation and its political timidity as to our capacity to regulate markets and to compensate for market failure. Mainstream economists, mainstream commentators and policy-makers alike convinced themselves that the market was synonymous with economic efficiency and was essentially self-regulating. As a consequence, there was little if anything that the state was capable of providing that was not better delivered through the free play of market mechanisms. This, of course, had consequences. Particularly insidious was the conviction (genuinely held, however misguided) that market-based systems of allocation were technically more efficient and that dynamic markets (particularly those characterized by financial innovation) were both so rapidly evolving as to be incapable of effective regulation and, more conveniently still, were self-equilibrating anyway. It was precisely this combination of assumptions that led so many on the centre-left, just as much as more natural enthusiasts on the right, to the view that widening social and economic inequality was a necessary and acceptable price to pay for the growth with which it was (assumed to be) associated.

What is more, this view led, almost by default, to a form of 'trickle-down' economics (see, for instance, Aghion and Bolton 1997). If markets were inherently efficient, then regulation (like any other form of state intervention) would merely suppress the potential for growth. Consequently, the optimal strategy was to free up the market in order to maximize the possibility of profitable accumulation – and to worry about the distributional consequences later. Of course, the political left worried much more than the right about the inegalitarian price paid for aggregate wealth maximization (or what passed in its name). Such anxieties took the form, in part, of concerns (and, somewhat less frequently, substantive policy innovations) about the state's societal obligation to provide more equal access to the market and to redistribute the proceeds of growth. But the problem was that any such redistribution was itself a form of state interference in the market and, hence, within the terms of the prevailing consensus, a source of inefficiency and a drain on growth and wealth.

Finally, and perhaps most worryingly (at least with the benefit of hindsight), such genuine anxieties led in an apparently more comforting direction. Here, the familiar refrain was that, even if its proceeds were unfairly distributed, since growth was so much greater than it would otherwise have been, the poor would still be better off – in absolute, if not in relative, terms. Widening inequality was, in short, the best that could be achieved – a necessary correlate of growth maximization. But, as we now know all too well, we had allowed ourselves to be duped. Many really did think that we had 'no alternative'; that market-conforming policies were good for us, for *all* of us; that markets were the best guarantors of the provision of collective public goods; that the algebraic alchemy of mainstream economic theory was all-seeing and could deliver the elixir of growth indefinitely – in sum, that the whole ideological framework of Anglo-liberalism did indeed underpin a stable and sustainable model of both competitiveness and growth (and, moreover, one that could be exported to the rest of the world).

That was then. We now know *all* of this to be wrong – and this revelation has profound consequences for how we think about ideology now. We highlight three lessons in particular as crucial for the civic capitalist alternative we propose. The first is that we must be far, far more wary of technocracy, managerialism and expert elitism. This is not how we have tended to think of our relationship with economic orthodoxy (the orthodoxy of the mainstream macroeconomic theory that informs so much of our policy-making); but it is exactly how we must now understand our political dependence on mainstream economic theory. Economics, as the crisis reveals, is never a science (at least, not in the lay sense of the term) and economic expertise is, as a consequence, a potentially dangerous thing. It is something that needs to be exercised carefully, held to account democratically and acknowledged for the political intervention that it always represents. Above all, we need to be aware of its inherent limitations – and not so easily taken in by the comforting thought that, although it is clearly a very difficult science, it is at least conducted (for the most part) by very intelligent people.

The second lesson follows directly from this. For once we acknowledge that markets are neither self-regulating nor self-equilibrating and that, as a consequence, market conformity is not so much the key to growth as the guarantor that any such growth is ultimately unsustainable, then the world looks very different. The state now emerges as integral to growth and, perhaps more significantly, to the sustainability of such growth. For it is the only body capable of regulating the market and such regulation is both the only means by which capitalism's propensity for crisis can be held in check and the only means by which the market can be made to answer to the citizens it ostensibly serves. The state (perhaps particularly in Britain) might not always have a very good record in market regulation and the dangers of state failure should not and cannot be understated or overlooked. But we simply cannot afford to assume that markets contain the capacity to regulate themselves and, in so doing, allow them in effect to regulate us. We need, in short, to remember our responsibility to regulate markets and to learn to be better regulators.

The third lesson is a correlate of the first two. As soon as we acknowledge that the state is, in effect, the public goods provider of last resort (the only body to which we can turn when the market fails), then we start to acknowledge its moral and political responsibility to us – as citizens. The state, in and through the governments we elect and in and through our capacity to hold them to account democratically, has a responsibility to us all to govern, manage and regulate the market economy and to deliver, in the process, outcomes we consider just and fair. The market is never and can never be a guarantor of equity or justice. Consequently, if we are to have social and economic justice, it has to be imposed upon the market by the state in our name.

That is the very nature of civic capitalism – the governance of the market, by the state, in the name of the people, to deliver collective public goods, equity and social justice. However, for such a civic capitalism to be possible, we have first to believe widely that this is possible, desirable and indeed necessary. This, to be clear, does not entail that we adopt a new statist ideology by which we entrust to the state without question all that we previously assumed the market would provide for itself. But it does mean that we need consciously to move on from the old ideological certainties (of the benign and self-equilibrating nature of market rationality, for instance). Instead, we need to espouse a different and a more open-ended set of values and ambitions, a different ideology in effect – one of civic, indeed democratic, economic governance. Together, as citizens of a democratic society, we need to ask not what we can do for the market, but what we wish the market to do for us. This is, then, the first, and in many ways the most fundamental, building block of a new civic capitalism.

State Intervention in the Market as a Civic Duty

Clearly, if we are to have a new capitalism worthy of the name, it must be a different capitalism to the one we have. As we have already suggested, this necessitates a different, and for us a more extensive and interventionist, role for the state. There are two obvious reasons for this. First, it is not possible to make the transition from one model of capitalism to another without the guiding hand of the state. Capitalism – as we now know but should really have known all along – does not put right its own pathologies (or not very many of them, to be sure). It does not auto-correct – it cannot 'rebalance' itself – and to think otherwise is to delude ourselves. Second, and no less significantly, the capitalism we have had is one in which the market has been in the ascendancy. We have conspired to produce, and subsequently come to suffer from, a capitalism unregulated, a capitalism unqualified, a capitalism left to its own devices, and one in which good outcomes could arise only serendipitously through benign neglect.

This will no longer do; we need to bring capitalism to account and that means building a new capitalism – a capitalism with an adjective, and one that *we* specify. And the reality is that the addition of an adjective, almost regardless of which adjective, entails state coordination – not just regulation, but regulation *for a societal purpose*. Our chosen adjective is 'civic' – we argue, as we have made clear, for a civic capitalism, a capitalism rebuilt to answer to the collective needs of the citizens it properly should serve (and should be made to serve).

The initial case, at least, for state intervention is easily made in the context of the crisis. For when banks go under, we recognize that we have a collective public interest in ensuring that the logic of the market does not prevail – the logic by which the innocent become victims, losing all of their savings in the process. It is in moments like this that we rediscover an implicit political logic that for too long we have preferred to ignore – that the state is the collective or public goods provider of last resort. When the market fails, when the bank goes under, it is the only authority to which we can turn; it is the sole guarantor of our security – financial, social or, indeed, environmental. If there is to be any kind of justice in such moments, it can only arise through the interventions of the state; markets, quite simply and quite literally, do not care.

The implications of this, when we start to think about them, are profound. For belated intervention in this way – bailing out the banks and underwriting them with government funds (nationalizing private debt) at the point of collapse – is very much the worst-case scenario. If the state had previously been trusted to engage in effective regulation of the market, and been competent in such regulation, then there would have been no need for such bailouts. And that is the point. A civic capitalism regulates the economy – and not just the banking sector – in the collective or public interest; it does not wait until a crisis strikes to intervene. But the argument here necessarily goes much further. This is not just about regulation to prevent unnecessary and dangerous risks being taken in the market which might compromise the life chances of those reliant on market actors. It is also about acknowledging that, at root, the market is both uncoordinated and uncoordinating – and, as such, is incapable of delivering collective public goods (for which read 'what we want as a society') in the absence of strong and coordinated governance.

One such public good, now increasingly widely acknowledged (and not just in Britain), is the need for an economy that is in some sense properly 'balanced' between different sectors and sources of growth. In Britain, of course, the debate has become especially focused on the urgent need for 'rebalancing', precisely because of the massive structural asymmetry between finance on the one hand and the productive economy on the other. Yet markets do not rebalance themselves, as the story of the British economy since the crisis manifestly shows (Berry 2013; Berry and Hay forthcoming). With the help of a targeted stimulus package (a palliative injected directly into the veins of the housing market), the unstable growth that characterized the pre-crisis bubble is back, however insecurely. Put differently, the growth we have today in Britain does not arise from 'rebalancing'. 'Rebalancing' needs concerted and sustained intervention and that we palpably lack.

But, in order for the state to take on that role, we need a different politics – one that can be trusted both to discern the public good and to act upon it – a politics that is more visible and more deliberative, and indeed more visibly deliberative, a politics that is more open to the wishes of those in whose name it intervenes. That is a very tall order in most advanced capitalist democracies today. Political reform needs to accompany economic reform; indeed, the former may well be a condition of the latter. The basic point is that we need to be able to trust the government, if not to do the right thing all of the time (which is impossible), then at least to do what it does for the right reasons and with genuine and defensible motives. And that, too, is a long way from where we are now.

This, in turn, suggests the need to articulate a clear set of principles capable of guiding government intervention in, and regulation of, the market in the managed transition to a more genuinely civic capitalism. We insist, in other words, that we must find ways to articulate a strong conception of the 'civic' in civic capitalism – a sense of social justice and injustice against which government interventions might be gauged (whether prospectively or retrospectively). But, in order for this to work, it needs to be combined with much greater visibility of the decision-making process, precisely so that we can all see, if we want to, that justice is indeed being done.

Specifying the content of such a conception of social justice is no easy task. From our perspective, there are two elements to this. The first is to outline a minimum set of values that we see as integral to the civic model of capitalism that we propose. The second is to generate the kind of societal debate about the model of capitalism we wish to build that the very notion of civic capitalism implies. For a civic capitalism worthy of the name entails a polity more open to the views of its citizens – a bringing of citizens into a more open political community. In terms of the former (the specification of core values), we would identify: equity, growth (or, better, economic development) whose dividends are more fairly and evenly shared, redistribution to correct market failure, economic and environmental sustainability, and a simple principle of international reciprocity (that we would not suffer if others did as we did). In terms of the latter, we need public deliberation, debate and consultation to draw out a set of societal or civic values that could guide the extent and purpose of the state intervention that is needed to construct and manage the type of capitalism we wish to build. This is a collective (and hence a civic) task – and one that is long overdue.

Regulation as the Only Antidote to Unstable Growth

One of the most important lessons of the global financial crisis is that we got – and indeed continue to get – regulation spectacularly wrong. For far too long we have thought of regulation simply as 'red tape' – an unnecessary imposition and an unwelcome and unwarranted interference leading, invariably, to tiresome, overbearing, cumbersome and inefficient bureaucracy. We inclined accordingly to as little of it as we could credibly get away with (the appropriate euphemism was 'light touch'). And, even if we carried a lingering doubt at the back of our minds about the probity of all of this, we comforted ourselves with the thought that this light-touch and market-conforming regulatory disposition was at least growth-enhancing – in that the blind eye it invariably cast on potentially rather shady practices almost certainly contributed to higher economic output and, in turn, to higher taxation receipts. It was, in other words, a 'win–win scenario'.

Shamed perhaps by their popular depiction as interfering meddlers pathologically predisposed to intrude into arenas they seldom understood (Hay 2007), the disposition of the regulators themselves was, far too often, also that of benign neglect. They, too, comforted themselves, this time with a slightly different thought – that markets, for the most part, were their own best regulators and market actors were in general better placed to assess the risks to which they exposed themselves than those seeking to second-guess their behaviour (Watson 2014). If that resulted in an historically high ratio of private debt to Gross Domestic Product (GDP), then so be it: the markets, and the actors who breathed life into them on a daily basis, surely knew what they were doing – and, above all, they were making money ... lots and lots of money (some of which was being recycled in taxation when it did not disappear offshore).

This was always wrong and it is an attitude and a disposition we can no longer afford as we seek to rebuild something better out of the ruins of the Anglo-liberal growth model. Interestingly, amongst the first to accept this and to call for a more precautionary regulatory disposition were many of the regulators themselves (or, at least, many of those on whose watch, as regulators, the crisis had unfolded – see, for instance, Bernanke 2011; Haldane and May 2011; King 2013). Chastened, presumably, by their experience and their incapacity at the time to prevent a slow-motion car crash unfolding before their eyes, many of them seem now to be of the view that the same cannot be allowed to happen again – and that, having in effect fallen asleep at the wheel once, it is their responsibility to ensure that those who replace them stay awake rather longer (and are liberally plied with caffeine to help them in this task).

Unfortunately, to date at least, they have not found a terribly receptive audience amongst those in the advanced political economies who appointed them as regulators in the first place. It is not difficult to understand why. The truth is that there was always something in the argument that regulation has a certain propensity to suppress growth – or, at least, some forms of growth. And growth is, of course, what incumbent administrations (particularly those seeking re-election) crave above all else. High loan-to-value ratios, low capital adequacy requirements, high levels of consumer debt, cheap credit, sub-prime lending and mortgage-backed securities all look like prime targets for a more precautionary regulatory regime. Yet, as long as the bubble lasted, each was a real source of growth – or, perhaps more accurately, a multiplier of potential growth.

Indeed, whether we like it or not, each has played a part in the putative 'recovery' of the British economy since the second quarter of 2013. That is precisely why such a recovery is spurious; it is not based on stable growth but rather the re-inflation of the bubble whose bursting precipitated the crisis in the first place. This is why we need appropriate regulation – market-steering or market-limiting regulation capable of precluding the re-inflation of asset-price bubbles such as we have seen in the housing market. But the point is that such regulation comes with a short-term price. For we have to accept that this kind of precautionary regulation is not consistent with the consumer debt-fuelled recovery prompted in Britain by the Coalition government since 2013; instead it entails, and must indeed be an integral part of, a transition to a new mode of development or growth for the British economy.

So what might such regulation entail? Consistent with the model of civic capitalism we are seeking to outline, we propose five principles for sound economic governance and a more practical rule of thumb. The five principles are simply stated:

1. First, and perhaps above all else, we argue that regulation should not just be about tempering market excess; it needs to serve, and be seen to serve, a wider societal purpose – to help markets contribute to the growth model of the economy as a whole.

2. Second, following Nobel Laureate Paul Krugman (2008, 2013), we suggest that regulation should be in proportion to the potential risk posed by the object of regulation. Krugman's focus here is the banking sector, but the

principle is more widely applicable. He argues that banks should be regulated not against universal and rigid rules, but in proportion to their systemic significance to the financial sector as a whole. Thus, we do not so much need a rule that precludes banks from becoming 'too big to fail' (or too big to be *allowed* to fail) so much as a regulatory regime which ensures both that banks too big to fail do not fail *and* that the burden of regulation they would endure is a strong disincentive to them ever attaining such a systemic significance in the first place.

3. Following almost directly from this, we suggest the need to adopt a principle of discretionary precaution in economic regulation. Effective regulation, whether of the energy market or the market for financial innovation, is most effective, not when it is rules-bound but when it is flexible, adaptive, intelligent and transparent. Regulators, as the crisis shows so effectively, need to be risk averse – even if at times that has the effect of closing off potentially lucrative investment or growth opportunities. They need, in other words, to adopt a strong and consistent precautionary principle. But they also need the authority to demand full and complete information disclosure from the institutions they regulate and a flexible capacity to respond dynamically to the risk assessments they generate on the basis of that information.

4. A further principle follows, with particular significance for complex and dynamic markets such as those for instruments of financial innovation. It is that, in the name of precautionary discretion, we should adopt a presupposition against financial innovation in the absence of a strong countervailing case. It is often argued that it is impossible to regulate financial markets effectively since financial market actors themselves are typically at least one step ahead of the regulators. There are usually two elements to the argument: first, that the almost constant innovation in financial instruments allows market actors to sidestep any regulatory rule or regime designed to hold them in check; second, and rather

unkindly, that those who regulate financial markets have typically failed to make money in them and, as a consequence, are not well placed to anticipate the creativity by which any rules they impose might be interpreted or circumvented. Although there may be an element of truth in both propositions, this only becomes an impediment to effective regulation of financial markets if we have a presupposition of tolerance to financial innovation. This can and should be overturned.

5. Finally, we suggest that regulation (whether domestic, international or global) is best seen as a collective public good. As such, it needs to be delivered through a system that is both public, on the one hand, and publicly accountable, on the other. Credit rating provides an excellent example and should be seen as part of the system of global regulation of markets and market risk. For credible and effective credit rating is categorically a public good – insofar as it serves either to reduce the risk to which financial investors expose themselves or helps them better to assess and hence hedge against that risk. But, as the dynamics of the crisis showed so clearly, we cannot entrust such an important task to private ratings agencies with a clear financial stake in the assets they rate and with little or no retrospective responsibility and accountability for the public good they ostensibly provide. The reality is that there are a range of public or quasi-public bodies which could take on such a role. For example, with respect to the credit rating of sovereign debt, the International Monetary Fund (IMF) in its periodic reporting in effect already provides credit ratings (just ones not expressed in the standard metric form). It is surely time to dispense altogether with private credit rating as we strive to build more appropriate public structures for the regulation of the global economy.

This brings us to a more practical concluding consideration. Regulators need to be trained in disequilibrium thinking. As we argued earlier, mainstream economic theory today is, almost exclusively, equilibrium theory. In other words, whatever its value and whatever its influence, it has virtually no capacity to prepare us for disequilibrium outcomes – like crises. Most of the time that is fine; but regulation is there to prepare us for, and thus guard us against, the possibility of catastrophic events. Regulators, in short, need to assume the worst; they cannot afford to presume the best. That perhaps also implies that we need to be recruiting regulators from previously unlikely places – and certainly not exclusively from amongst a cadre of neoclassically trained equilibrium theorists.

The Need for Sustainability

As we have already insisted, the civic capitalism we advocate is very different from the capitalism we are used to. One of the biggest differences and one of the greatest challenges is that any aspirationally civic capitalism needs to prove itself to be sustainable – economically, institutionally *and* environmentally. The present crisis is a crisis of an unstable growth model and, at the same time, a more general crisis of the model of capitalism of which the former was an expression. But, even in the absence of the crisis, Anglo-liberal capitalism (like most capitalisms) was – as it remains – environmentally unsustainable. The crisis has perhaps made it easier to see what was already the case – namely, the urgent need to find a more genuinely sustainable model of capitalism and associated societal development. But the condition long predates the crisis. None of these challenges is easy, but that of ensuring environmental sustainability is undoubtedly the hardest.

Yet there are a number of things than can – and perhaps must – be said on this critical issue. First, there is a need for a certain modesty and humility in the face of the challenge and the choice we face. The brutal point is that we have done nothing – or nothing very significant – for far, far too long. Whether we failed to try hard enough or tried hard and failed is a moot point, but it is also now largely academic.

We simply cannot afford not to try harder now – and, indeed, to succeed. And that means a grim realism with respect to our plight, combined with a sense of the magnitude of our inter-generational responsibility. In a way, the crisis might prepare us well for that. But, in another sense, this is obviously not a good time to turn our attention to the environmental crisis, especially if that means facing up to the problem of growth itself. The hard truth is that it is clearly more difficult to make the case for less growth, or an alternative to growth as the global metric of economic performance, at precisely the moment when growth appears so hard to achieve in our own economies. But that is precisely what we need to do – and we need to do so successfully and on an international stage.

A second point is that we can no longer afford the indulgence and evasion of climate change denial. Whether malevolent and duplicitous or more simply a product of ignorance or wishful thinking, it can no longer be tolerated. If we think in terms of the planet's 'carrying capacity', then the evidence is unequivocal – and unequivocally appalling. To think in such terms is to start to gauge current planetary resource use in terms of the safe operating space for humanity with respect to the earth's biophysical sub-systems. And what is startlingly clear is that, when we start to counter-pose current figures on environmental degradation with expert 'best approximations' of the planet's carrying capacity (the point beyond which we simply cannot go without threatening human life, certainly as we know it, on earth), we find again and again that we have already reached the tipping point. The results are summarized in the table below for a small subset of the planetary carrying capacities we might consider.

Data like this show that we are already in the red zone (where current levels exceed planetary carrying capacity, the darker shading) with respect to a number of earth-system processes and are moving rapidly into the red zone in the others. Of that much we can be sure. And such data are merely reinforced if we change perspective somewhat and

Earth system processes	Parameter	Boundary	Current level
Climate change	Atmospheric CO_2 (ppm)	350	>400
Biodiversity loss	Extinction rate (no. of species per million per year)	10	>100
Nitrogen cycle	Amount of nitrogen removed from the atmosphere for human use (million tonnes per year)	35	>120
Freshwater use	Human consumption of freshwater (km^3 per year)	4000	c. 3000
Ocean acidification	Global mean saturation state of aragonite in surface sea water	2.75	2.9
Landmass usage	Per cent of global landmass used for crops	15	c. 12

Source: Adapted and updated from Rockström et al. 2009.

look not at the planet's carrying capacity but our own eco-logical footprint. This measures, in effect, the land and sea mass necessary to support the resources a human population (such as a nation) consumes and to absorb the waste it pro-duces. The most recent figures from the WWF's *Living Planet Report* (2012) show that the world average ecological footprint (2.7 global hectares per person) exceeds available land and sea mass (2.1 global hectares per person) by over 30 per cent. The figures for Britain and the United States are, respectively, 4.7 and 7.2 global hectares per person; that for Haiti, by stark comparison, is a mere 0.6.

A third point – and one that has a certain irony in the context of our wider argument – is that things would actually be worse still but for the global financial crisis. It is not often that one can say that but, with respect to the environment, it is true. The crisis has arguably done more to reduce the pace (or at least slow the acceleration) of the process of global environmental degradation than anything directly intended to have such an effect. And that is because it has served to reduce aggregate global growth rates.

Yet we need to proceed with some caution here. For one's enemies' enemies do not always make good friends – and we can have environmentally unsustainable non-growth just as much as we can have environmentally unsustainable growth. Indeed, the story of the crisis is a story of the move from the latter to the former ... and perhaps back again. What such reflections remind us is how crucial the question of growth is to our capacity to respond to the challenge of the environmental crisis. Almost certainly, we will need to come to think of growth in rather different terms if we are to do anything at all to take us out of the red zone (and the time-lag effects, it need scarcely be pointed out, are very considerable indeed).

So how might we do this? For there are undoubtedly things we can do and we need to do them urgently – thinking, while we do so, of our duty of care to future generations. One of these is, on the face of it, deceptively simple (though one should not underestimate the political difficulties of what we here propose). It is that we should work collectively and globally to change the accepted currency of economic success, replacing the *convention* of growth (for that is what in essence it is) with something else, albeit something more complicated. In this process, we need to devise a measure or index based on a more balanced and sustainable array of genuinely global (indeed, planetary) collective public goods whose promotion might eventually replace the blind and narrow pursuit of economic output as *the* global currency of economic success.

The point here is that it is not difficult to imagine what might be entailed in such an exercise. Alongside GDP data, we would need to build a new index of economic success – a compound index, inevitably, which might include things like changes in the Gini coefficient (in the direction of greater societal equality), changes in per capita energy use (rewarding increased energy efficiency and sustainability), changes in per capita carbon emissions and other planetary boundary statistics (rewarding the greening of residual growth) and perhaps a range of more basic development indices (changes in literacy rates and so forth). This alternative social, environmental and developmental or sustainable economic development (SED) index (either will suffice, for now, as a working title) would be recorded and published alongside GDP and would thus allow the production of a new hybrid GDP-SED index. Over a globally agreed timescale, the proportion of SED relative to GDP in the hybrid index would rise – from zero (now) to close to 100 per cent (at some agreed point in the future). And, of course, we would gauge whether our economies were 'growing', 'flatlining' or 'in recession' according to the new hybrid index as, in effect, we moved from measuring economic performance in terms of GDP to measuring it in terms of SED.

The changes to our modes of living, over that period of time, would be immense – and would need to be immense. And they would be accompanied by a new set of roles for a new set of international institutions. In the process, structural adjustment would be decisively recast – no longer the mantra of neoliberal labour-market reform and privatization but, instead, the reorientation of economies to promote sustainability according to the SED index. This may seem like a long way off – and it is. But if we are even to begin to rectify our planetary imbalance, it is imperative – a necessary, but of course far from sufficient, condition of exiting the red zone.

But – and here we come to a crucial point – is the implication of this that we should abandon the search for growth today? Our answer is 'no': in fact, quite the contrary. What is required is a massive public investment in sustainable technologies and new public infrastructure (in transport as much as anything else). This can and will bring growth. But, far more importantly, it will create the resources that might allow us to make the transition to a more sustainable conception of societal and economic development and, in so doing, to build a capitalism better able to meet the long-term needs and ambitions of the citizens it must be made to serve.

Sustainable Development through Investment

A most urgent task for any newly elected or, indeed, re-elected British government is to fix the growth model. Since the early 1990s, Britain experimented, in effect, with a new kind of growth model, which we have termed Anglo-liberal and others 'privatized Keynesianism' (Crouch 2008, 2011; Hay 2011, 2013; Watson 2010). That model, as we have argued, was always unsustainable. Indeed, its pathologies were not difficult to discern for those willing to look for them. It relied on a low-inflation/low-interest rate equilibrium that could never endure indefinitely and it generated, on the back of that, a series of asset-price bubbles. The global financial crisis was, in large part, a story of the bursting of such bubbles – not just in Britain – and the transmission globally of the contagion through a variety of instruments of financial intermediation which had allowed banks and other financial institutions to take a stake in Anglo-liberal growth (Gamble 2014).

In particular, as is now widely accepted, Britain's highly distinctive and, for well over two decades, largely successful growth model was based on the nurturing of a culture of conspicuous private consumption fuelled by ever-rising levels of consumer debt. What made this possible was a combination of low interest rates, a competitive market for consumer credit and pervasive private housing tenure – the origins of each of which can be traced further back to the monetarist revolution, the demutualization of mortgage provision (and the wider deregulation of financial services) and the extension of private home ownership in the early 1980s respectively. With such factors in place, this model generated sustained (if, ultimately, unsustainable) growth for nearly a quarter of a century, though at a relatively modest level in comparative historical terms.

Low interest rates reduced the effective cost of home ownership, though this had the side effect of increasing demand in the housing market and hence prices. Ultimately, it was house price inflation on which the growth model was predicated – albeit, initially, without any conscious or deliberate strategy to promote it. For in a low interest rate world with low returns on savings, all the incentives – for those who could afford it – were to enter a rising housing market at the first opportunity. The housing market became an independent source of wealth for those able to run with it and, more importantly, a privileged point of access to credit for those prepared to release the equity accumulating in their home to fuel their increasingly addictive consumption habit.

In this way, asset appreciation and equity release became integral to growth. This is what is meant by 'privatized Keynesianism' (Crouch 2011) – the heart of the Anglo-liberal growth model. Private debt – in the form of credit typically secured against property – became a demand stimulus to the economy, allowing higher levels of consumption, employment and growth than would otherwise have been the case. But this was always a fragile growth model. For it could only last so long as the low-inflation/low-interest-rate equilibrium persisted. And, in the run-up to the crisis, this was shattered by steep rises in oil prices, reinforced by speculation in oil futures markets. The resulting interest rate hikes crashed first the American and then the British housing markets. The rest, as they say, is history – painfully recent history, but history all the same.

So what are the implications of this today? These come in two kinds – some immediate ones for the recent return to growth in Britain and some longer-term ones for the wider project of building a more sustained and more sustainable recovery consistent with the transition to a more genuinely civic capitalism not only in Britain but also across a number of advanced industrial countries.

The first implication is that, as we have already argued, Britain's current recovery is largely an illusion and is dangerously unsustainable. Growth has, indeed, returned to the British economy since 2013. Yet this is a growth based on resuscitating, at least temporarily, the old unsustainable model of growth. The banks have been recapitalized with public funds and actively encouraged, through the 'Funding for Lending' and 'Help to Buy' schemes, for instance, to refocus and re-concentrate the supply of credit on the housing market – and with some success. House prices are rising, at least in the south-east of Britain. But the reality is that this is an inherently risky strategy – and one that is only imaginable in the short term (a pre-election gambit perhaps). The housing market is in fact significantly overvalued, even after the recalibration of the crisis (especially if one looks at the question of affordability inter-generationally and at likely medium-term trends in interest rates). This means that we are dancing on the edge of the precipice again.

So what might a different incoming government in Britain do to put this right? Five practical implications follow directly from our analysis, each contributing to the transition from an unsustainable model of debt-fuelled growth to a more sustainable investment-led model of development.

1. *Politicizing the cost of borrowing.* If the economy is to be 'rebalanced', then the government and the Bank of England need to be putting concerted downward pressure on the actual cost of borrowing (independent of the base rate), particularly in sectors where a clear link to the growth strategy for the economy can be made and substantiated. The banks have in effect been allowed to recapitalize themselves by charging commercial borrowers, mortgage holders and those servicing consumer debt a sizeable interest-rate premium, relative to the base rate, to compensate for their huge investment banking losses during the crisis. This is both intolerable and a significant drain on the growth prospects of the commercial and consumer economy. It has been said before, but remains true: the banks need to be named and shamed and held publicly to account for their behaviour.

2. *From private to public investment.* Whilst such
interest-rate premiums persist, there is a strong argument to
be made not just for private but for public investment
in support of a clearly articulated growth strategy built on
identifying and supporting a series of key export-oriented
sectors. The cost of financing long-term public borrowing is
significantly lower than for commercial lenders. Moreover,
public infrastructure projects are likely to be critical to
any reconfiguration of the economy towards a new (and
more clearly export-oriented) growth strategy. Public
investment – especially in infrastructure renewal – can be
a highly cost-effective way of providing the public goods
on which the transition to a new model of growth relies.

3. *Hypothecated investment or growth bonds.* How
might such investment be funded? There are many options
which might be considered, but one is the use of public
investment or growth bonds – a form of hypothecated government debt and, in effect, an ethical form of investment available to financial institutions and private citizens
alike. The funds secured in this way would be earmarked
for public infrastructural projects and might be distributed
through a range of national or regional investment banks.
In addition to infrastructure, these might fund sustainable technologies and the human capital to utilize such
technologies.

4. *Conditional deficit and debt reduction.* A further
implication of the analysis presented here is that we cannot
afford to consider deficit reduction as a goal in itself – and
certainly not the principal goal guiding economic policy.
Deficit reduction in a context of stagnant or negative growth
is suicidal and threatens only to produce a vicious circle of
declining economic output. But this is not to suggest that
there is a simple choice to be made between deficit reduction
and growth promotion – but rather that deficit reduction
must be made conditional on growth. Any incoming British
government would need not only to be clear about its

strategy for securing growth, but also to make a strong, and public, pre-commitment to an explicit growth target and a linked, sliding, scale of deficit reduction (the greater the growth rate attained, the greater the deficit and debt reduction). This is the only way to ensure that deficit and debt reduction writ large does not even now turn a global crisis into a global recession in a manner analogous to the 1930s.

5. *International coordination of debt and growth management.* The economic case for conditional deficit and debt reduction is a very strong one, but it undoubtedly has its political difficulties. To announce the end of deficit reduction in one economy alone, especially in the current ideological climate and in a context of the timidity of financial institutions, would threaten a run on the currency and a steep rise in the cost of servicing (short-term) national debt. Consequently, it is imperative that steps are taken at an international (and, ideally, a global or at least Group of 20 (G20)) level to agree a coordinated strategy for managing debt and growth, as well as, in time, for moving away from the crude notion of output growth as the predominant currency of economic performance.

These five points do not in themselves constitute a sustainable model of economic development for Britain or anywhere else, but they remain necessary steps in the direction of civic capitalism.

Towards an Alternative Currency of Global Economic Success

As we have been at pains to show, the model of growth enjoyed by the British economy for the two decades before the crisis and the broader model of capitalism out of which it arose were always inherently unsustainable – economically, politically ... but also environmentally. The first and second sources of this instability are now widely appreciated and they feature prominently in the still ongoing and largely

unresolved discussion of alternative future scenarios. But the
third, though also well understood, is typically forgotten at
precisely the moment that talk turns from crisis definition to
potential solutions to our economic woes. That will not do.
For the crisis gives us the opportunity – a rare, even unprec-
edented, opportunity – to reflect on and begin to put right
all that is broken in our political economic model.

Above all, this means focusing on the steps required to
build a civic capitalism that is environmentally sustainable.
And this, in turn, means thinking about growth in a rather
different way and posing some disarming and troubling
questions. The first is exceptionally simply stated: is environmentally sustainable growth possible? Yet what is remarkable is how seldom that question is ever directly posed. In a
sense, it haunts progressive political economy – which, for
the most part, would like to think of itself as green and yet
at the same time seems decidedly (if often implicitly) pro-
growth. We tend to assume (conveniently) that we can have
environmentally sustainable growth and (even more conveniently) that, when we talk of growth (and of the strategies
to attain or restore it), this is the kind of growth that we
have in mind. But that will not do any longer: not least
because, as we have already shown, humanity is now at an
environmental crossroads, having exceeded in an alarming
number of ways the planet's carrying capacity.

The story of our environmental crisis is the story, amongst
other things, of symbolic breaches. On 10 May 2013, the
Earth Systems Research Laboratory (an environmental
observatory and part of the US National Oceanic and Atmos-
pheric Administration), perched 11,000 feet up atop the
Mauna Loa volcano in Hawaii, recorded its first ever average
daily carbon dioxide level in excess of 400 parts per million
(ppm) – the latest such breach (Carrington 2013). CO_2 last
reached such levels some 5 million years ago! 400 ppm, just
like every other such symbolic ceiling, was long considered
an unattainable figure, a level we could simply not allow
ourselves to hit – a kind of doomsday portent and the point
at which we would need to become (if we were not already)

very, very scared that the damage we had inflicted on the planet was likely to prove irreparable and irreversible. But it came and went, just like all the others, and most of us no longer give it very much thought. Indeed, we are becoming increasingly immune to such symbolic breaches – they lose their shock value as we become ever more familiar with the process of environmental and ecological grieving. The truth is, however, that we cannot carry on like this and, at heart, most of us now know that – even perhaps those who seek a kind of temporary solace in climate change denial (though maybe that is too generous to them).

So where does this analysis take us? A potentially fruitful way to think about this is in terms of the 'carbon footprint of growth'. If we acknowledge that all growth has a carbon footprint – and that is perhaps as close to a truism as anything in this extended thought-experiment – then that suggests three potential types of response. We might seek to offset the carbon footprint (though, of course, that cannot work at a planetary level); we might seek to reduce the carbon footprint (by making our growth less environmentally damaging than it might otherwise be); or we might strive to reduce our dependence on growth and to promote other measures of economic success. Of these, it is the third, we think, which holds out the greatest prospect of realization, although, interestingly, it is the least discussed. Growth, in a way, is a convention for measuring economic success. Indeed, it has become the global currency of economic success. And it is not difficult to see why. But all conventions can be rethought – and there is a very strong moral and ecological argument for suggesting that growth should no longer be tolerated as the global standard by which economic performance is gauged. *Things could and can be different.* But what we almost certainly cannot do is to replace GDP growth at a stroke with some other measure of economic success; the transition would need to be managed carefully and cumulatively, and coordinated globally.

The basic idea for this has already been introduced. We described earlier how an alternative compound index (what we termed the social, environmental and developmental, or the sustainable economic development (SED) index) might slowly come to replace GDP as the international standard of economic performance and development. Here, we explain in a little more detail – in five simple points – the underlying logic, what this might entail and how the transition might be made.

1. GDP is a simple but perverse measure of economic performance, especially in a context in which the planet's very carrying capacity is being exceeded. For it encourages environmental resource depletion and rewards population growth whilst giving no consideration either to the environmental externalities of output growth or the capacity of an economy to meet the needs of its citizens. In this latter respect, even GDP per capita is an improvement. But, ultimately, neither can be tolerated much longer as the global currency of economic success and the most basic measure of economic performance.

2. But, if we are to replace GDP with an alternative and more sustainable measure of economic performance, it must be a more complex or compound index – an index, in effect, comprised of the weighted aggregation of a series of different indices. For it is only in this way that we can hope to capture in a single measure the various respects in which different and distinct national capitalisms can and must be made to answer to the needs and aspirations of their citizens. This is what we mean by civic capitalism.

3. Some of those elements – and hence some of the measures within the index – are integral to the very notion of civic capitalism in so far as they relate to core collective public goods and the satisfaction of basic human needs. Amongst these, we have already identified measures of social inequality (rewarding reductions in Gini coefficients, for instance), measures of health and basic welfare (rewarding, perhaps, improvements in life expectancy and reductions in

the spread of life expectancies within a nation), changes in per capita energy use (rewarding increased energy efficiency and sustainability), changes in per capita carbon emissions and other planetary boundary statistics (rewarding the greening of economic activity) and perhaps a range of more basic development indices (rewarding improvements in literacy and numeracy rates and so forth). Yet, in the spirit of the civic capitalism we are seeking to build, other elements might more appropriately emerge out of consultation and domestic deliberation involving citizens themselves. The point is that there is space for quite a lot in a compound SED index of this kind.

4. Yet this must, in the end, become a global index. Whilst individual political economies might well, in the first instance, wish to develop their own SEDs to measure and capture progress with respect to the values they are seeking to incorporate within their own civic capitalisms (and should actively be encouraged to do so), GDP needs to be replaced at a global level. This requires international coordination by new, or newly enabled, agents of global economic and environmental governance (either a revamped IMF or World Bank or a new agency designed for the purpose). In that sense, what is required is the development of such indices domestically by governments willing and able to make the case for them as global indices on an international stage.

5. Crucially, too, we must acknowledge that the transition from GDP to SED as the global currency of economic success cannot be instantaneous or rapid. It needs to be managed carefully and coordinated internationally. We have some time perhaps to get this right, but we do need to start very soon.

What, finally, will be the consequences of such a transition for 'growth' as we know it now? That will depend in part on the specific contents of the SED index we settle on. But it is important to stress that the transition from GDP to SED does not mean a complete end to growth in conventional terms – even if it does mean an end to the fetishization of such growth as an end in itself. Indeed, for many poorer 'developing' economies in Africa, Asia and Latin America to progress at all in SED, they will need to grow significantly *as well* in GDP and GDP per capita terms. What it does almost certainly require, however, is a more equitable distribution of the dividends of any such global growth. That, ultimately, is the test of whether civic capitalism can become global civic capitalism.

Bringing in the Social Dimension

We have focused so far on the political and economic aspects of the flawed, and now failed, Anglo-liberal model of capitalist development and of the 'civic capitalist' alternative that we have been setting out. But political economy, both as analysis and practice, does need also fully to embrace the 'social' dimension – much more so in fact than it usually does – and it is time now to turn to this aspect of the discussion directly.

There has, of course, always been a concept of the social bound up within the liberal model. It is familiar to us and is grounded in the notion of the rational, egotistical, self-seeking individual charting his or her way through life, unencumbered by awareness of conditioning by society, let alone being ready and willing to bear responsibility for participating in it and ensuring its wider collective functioning. In Britain at least, the idea was captured in Mrs Thatcher's observation that 'there is no such thing as society'. Whilst her remarks were, in a sense, taken out of context, the famous shortened quote is important. It has endured precisely because it encapsulates so brilliantly an attitude to the social that was (sadly) emblematic of neoliberal thinking not only in Britain itself but worldwide. In a nutshell, the view was that the social dimension in political economy need not be thought about or attended to because it was a given that individual ambition, decision-making and strategy were at the heart of all things. Look after the political and the economic (above all, make the political answer to the economic) and the social will look after itself. How wrong can one be?

Of course, this will not do in civic capitalism, almost by definition. For, in this model, those selfish and free-standing individuals are transmuted into citizens with real rights and responsibilities. They constitute the society that capitalism must be made to serve. Indeed, we have already recognized this by calling for the development of a new international standard of economic performance beyond GDP to be known as the SED index. In this frame of reference, the key questions then become the following: how best to think through the social; how to incorporate such an understanding into a new model; and what to draw on intellectually to do so? There are various possible answers and they have varying merits.

One seemingly plausible move would be to turn to the concept of the 'quality of life', understood as a means of taking the discussion beyond notions of standard of living to embrace more qualitative indicators. Some of the work undertaken on this terrain is now based on 'life evaluations', wherein individuals are asked to assess and self-score their life on a scale in relation to certain specified experiences. It is unquestionably interesting and has opened up a lively enough debate about happiness, which even includes attempts to measure Gross National Happiness! But, in general, the life evaluation approach is descriptive, rather than prescriptive, and does not connect that well to the political arena.

Globally, the most widely used means of assessing the quality of life within countries is the Human Development Index (HDI) developed over many years by the United Nations Development Programme (UNDP) on the basis of Amartya Sen's (1993) work on the capabilities and functionalities of human beings. In a nutshell, the HDI is worked out by combining three measures of development: a long and healthy life; an education index that measures the extent of schooling; and a decent standard of living. One of us (Payne

2013) has written about this in more detail previously. Again, it is very interesting and certainly more subtle than measurement solely by reference to GDP. It comes up as well with some striking anomalies – the shaming fact, for example, that Britain, although the sixth largest economy in the world, could only crawl its way to twenty-sixth in the world in the HDI rankings in 2013.

Another recent attempt to develop a better way to incorporate the social into the practice of political economy appeared in the 2009 Report of the Commission on the Measurement of Economic Performance and Social Progress. This was headed by Nobel Laureates Amartya Sen (appearing again in our story) and Joseph Stiglitz and facilitated by the French economist Jean-Paul Fitoussi, following a commendable initiative to establish such an inquiry by then President Sarkozy of France. However, the Report itself has been widely considered to be disappointing. As its title revealingly indicated, it separated the economic and social arenas according to the common practice that it was perhaps invited to challenge. All in all, its work has been judged by many of those working in the social indicators field as constituting 'old wine in new skins' (Noll 2011).

The truth is that the quality of life concept, although intuitively appealing as a potential new lodestar on this front, is rendered inadequate for our purposes precisely because it does not take us beyond a focus on the individual and his or her psychological assessment of their life experiences, no matter how much they are set up to embrace. In other words, social progress is defined only as the sum of the satisfactions, or otherwise, of all of the individual members of society.

For our purposes, it is preferable to draw on an approach that is more social (and, indeed, sociological) in flavour and inspiration, namely, the work being done by several scholars to assess the 'social quality' of society more generally. This derived initially from a book jointly published by W. L. Beck, Laurent van der Maesen and Alan Walker (1997) in the late

1990s as part of a project initiated by the European Foundation for Social Quality (EFSQ).

In classic sociological fashion, social quality thinking conceives of society as providing the context for the exercise of individual agency and is thus able immediately to distinguish between societal and individual well-being (although recognizing that the two are inextricably linked). This, of itself, is an important step forward. The approach then goes on to identify the four main aspects of social quality:

- socio-economic security, meaning that people must have the resources over time to cope with daily life in dignity, both in adverse and good times;
- social cohesion, understood as the glue that binds society together and builds trust amongst its participants;
- social inclusion, referring to the degree to which people are, and feel, integrated into institutions, organizations, groups of friends and kinship systems;
- social empowerment, defined as the capacity of people to take advantage of the opportunities open to them as citizens and associated in consequence not only with their levels of education and health but also their subjective feelings about the extent and nature of their agency within society.

This is certainly an attractive package of ideas, although it still needs, and is rightly getting from its advocates, more elaboration and detail. Much of the current work of the EFSQ is now devoted to cross-European measurement of existing social quality in different countries. This is manifestly important in research terms, but it is to be hoped that the search for quantitative refinement does not excessively trump the conceptual development of the idea itself.

The reason for saying this is that it is immediately apparent that an embrace of the concept of social quality puts on the table a whole series of potential social policies that could be appropriate parts of a new civic capitalist model. These should really be taken forward by social policy specialists, rather than the two of us, but consider, for now, the merits of asking, and then answering effectively, some of the following questions. Should not economic policy in future be evaluated, at least in part, by what it does for the autonomy and agency of those experiencing it? Do mass lay-offs, as opposed to shared working in recessionary times, look quite the same from this perspective? Could not labour market and employment policies be better designed to facilitate the participation of people in the enterprises to which they devote many hours of their life? Is it the case that social policies cannot be devised to foster social solidarity in particular contexts, as well as to prioritize human dignity in schools, hospitals and workplaces? In an internet age where so much raw information is so easily available, why cannot education policy be reframed to focus centrally on the gaining of a more meaningful sense of social empowerment by learners?

None of this is very radical. Yet it all flows from, and can be achieved within, a model of civic capitalism that sees the pursuit of social quality as a core and defining value. More detailed policy elaboration by appropriate specialists is clearly required to put some flesh on the bones highlighted above, but these bones must now be part of the new body, the new model of capitalism, that we need to build.

A Shared Commitment to Reduce Inequality

One of the few positive developments since the crisis has been the increased political salience of the question of pervasive inequality. Once the almost exclusive preoccupation of critics of contemporary capitalism, it has more recently emerged as a no less central concern of its staunchest defenders. *The Economist* magazine, always alert to the future prospects of and threats to the free market, ran a special feature on the inequality debate in October 2012 (Beddoes 2012). Then, in December 2013, President Barack Obama declared that the growing gap between rich and poor in the United States posed 'a fundamental threat to the American dream, our way of life and what we stand for around the globe' – so much so that reversing it had now become 'the defining challenge of our time' (Obama 2013). Most recently, in December 2013 in the run-up to its latest gathering in Davos, the World Economic Forum (2013) reported that its elite business members judged rising inequality to be the biggest threat to global prosperity over the next few years.

All of this is very revealing because, for a long time, for far too long in fact, advocates of the Anglo-liberal growth model were generally content to ignore the evidence of the growing inequality that was piling up around them. The rich got hugely and flagrantly richer. The middle was 'squeezed' as their incomes stagnated in real terms over a period of decades and the consumerist lifestyle on which the growth model relied was maintained by their growing dependence on debt. As Joseph Stiglitz (2013) put it so well, continuing growth became 'reliant on the bottom 80 percent consuming about 110 percent of their income'. At the bottom, the poor struggled and many dropped out of society. In general, very few mainstream analysts worried about what the picture as a whole looked like and it was widely conceded that inequality as a political issue just did not get off the ground.

That was then. Post-crisis, we surely ought to think differently. An Oxfam briefing paper, released in January 2014, shows in crisp fashion just how bad things have got globally in terms of inequality (Oxfam 2014). We summarize:

- Almost half of the world's wealth is now owned by just 1 per cent of the population.
- The wealth of the 1 per cent richest people in the world amounts to US$110 trillion. That is 65 times the total wealth of the bottom half of the world's population.
- The bottom half of the world's population owns the same as the richest 85 people in the world.
- Seven out of ten people live in countries where economic inequality has increased in the last 30 years.
- The richest 1 per cent increased their share of income in 24 out of 26 countries for which we have data between 1980 and 2012.

What is more, the situation has worsened extraordinarily since the crisis. Oxfam also reports on research carried out by Emmanuel Saez (2013) of the University of California, Berkeley, which shows that 'in the US, the wealthiest 1 per cent captured 95 per cent of post-financial crisis growth since 2009, while the bottom 90 per cent became poorer'. This is social and political dynamite – or at least it ought to be.

However, there is another – possibly even more important – point to be made here. Inequality is not just the unfortunate outcome of a flawed growth model or even the consequence of the failure of a flawed growth model. It was actually one of the *defining features* of that model, one of the core characteristics that fuelled it in its heyday and ultimately rendered it unbalanced and unstable. By allowing the rich to escape previously existing social constraints, by squeezing the middle and by further impoverishing the poor, inequality played a critical role in creating the very economic mess the crisis exposed and from which we have still to extricate ourselves.

What, then, does such an analysis mean for the citizens that we have placed at the heart of our attempt to delineate a new model of civic capitalism? Three quick and simple points immediately follow: that this level of inequality is morally offensive to our collective sense of humanity; that it is socially destructive, eroding trust, increasing mental and physical ill health and restricting social mobility; and that it is politically pernicious in the way it facilitates the 'political capture' of states by concentrations of wealth and corporate interests. These are crucial things to say. But, above all, we want to make, and work through, here a fourth, perhaps more complicated, point that is grounded fully in political economy. In a nutshell, we contend that, in addition, extreme inequality is economically damaging and actually undermines the stability and sustainability of capitalist development. A new model needs to be built upon a broader, more equal, social base in which the middle is not squeezed but instead 'settled', perhaps even 'satisfied' (in a bow to those like the Skidelskys (2012) who have recently and tellingly invited everyone to think about 'how much is enough').

Importantly, too, because of the central role it played in the generation of the crisis, inequality cannot be left on the back burner until growth is safely resumed. This would be to fall back again into the familiar economic argument that the question of efficiency has to be separated from considerations of equity. The idea here is that the size of the cake has to be expanded to the maximum before we think about how to share it, the worry being that any attempt to bring about redistribution is likely to affect growth negatively by interfering with incentives. We do not accept this, taking the contrary view that alleviating inequality and promoting sustainable growth, far from being antithetical, are actually deeply intertwined and completely complementary.

In effect, political economy needs to reflect again on the question of the degree to which inequality is a precondition of economic innovation and development. Our intuitive answer is that some inequality is probably necessary to ensure that there are sufficient incentives to invest, produce and work, but that anything like the kind of inequality we have become accustomed to living with in fact threatens the broad social base on which sound economic development depends. This argument was in fact grasped for most of the twentieth century by those far-sighted business leaders who understood that their workers needed sufficient remuneration for their labour to be able to buy the goods and services they were making. Put differently, they knew that you could not build successful capitalist development solely around the production and sale of yachts, expensive cars and luxury homes!

This insight was deployed to good effect by Joseph Stiglitz in early 1993 when he argued in *The New York Times* that there were four major reasons why inequality was 'squelching' the recovery. First, the middle class was 'too weak to support the consumer spending that has historically driven our economic growth'; second, the 'hollowing out of the middle class since the 1970s' meant that it could no longer afford to invest in its future; third, the loss of this middle income was 'holding back tax receipts', especially since those at the top were so adroit at avoiding taxes; and, fourth, inequality was associated with 'more frequent and more severe boom-and-bust cycles that make our economy more volatile and vulnerable'. This piece was much debated, and disagreed with even by fellow Keynesians. But Stiglitz was surely right to insist on the truthfulness and continuing relevance of a key element of Keynes's own economic theorizing, which was that middle- and lower-income citizens have a much higher marginal propensity to consume than the rich and very rich whom he considered to be more likely to save than spend their enormous earnings.

In short, we need to rebuild as swiftly as possible the broader spending base on which capitalism used to sit prior to the crazed rush towards the extreme inequality racked up over the past several decades in most advanced countries. What is more, we know how to do it because we have done it before – from the late 1930s onwards and into the post-1945 era. The methods are: progressive taxation of income and wealth; the serious pursuit of corporate tax avoidance on a coordinated, global basis; the enactment of proper policies to require the payment of living wages; the public provision of universal health care, education and social protection to citizens; and the defence of the rights of workers within the law to organize themselves inside trade unions.

Can it be done again in hard times post-crisis? That will depend in the end on politics and the courage and vision of political leaders. We have shown, however, that the political economy of a broader, more equal, social base would increase growth, generate more taxes, reduce welfare spending, free up resources to devote to public investments and, generally, create a virtuous circle of civic capitalist development. After all, what is there not to like if you are not a member of the 1 per cent that has benefited so much from the neoliberalism of the past several decades? It is sound political economy, and it is a better morality play than the one we have been participating in.

Locating the New Model within the Global Context

A new national model of civic capitalism has inevitably to be located and embedded in a global context. The extent and the complexity of the interdependence that has steadily grown between national economies and societies over the past half-century is such that this is now a truism, albeit one still too easily and too frequently overlooked in national policy debates. In fact, the kind of civic capitalism we propose would be stillborn were it to emerge and be thought of purely at a national level. 'Civic capitalism in one country' is an oxymoron. Or, put slightly differently, the conditions of existence of civic capitalism are not exclusively, nor perhaps even principally, domestic.

In the final substantive section of our argument, then, we turn to a vital question, one that in effect oversees the whole debate about the possibility of moving forward towards a civic capitalist model of development anywhere. This is the matter of how we think about, as a means to reconfigure, what is usually called the system of 'global governance'. By this, we refer simply to the loose mix of arrangements, institutions and rules that now exists at the global level with a view to giving some coherence and order to the diverse mix of policies and approaches to governance being followed across the many different states of the world.

The structures of global governance that we have inherited from the neoliberal era are actually very limited, both in scope and ambition. For some time, the dominant view judged that little more was required than effective rules for managing competition between national economies. From this perspective, the IMF provided surveillance of financial risk and maintained the stability of the international financial order; the World Bank offered technical and other support to the development efforts of the poorer countries; and the World Trade Organization (WTO) negotiated an (ostensibly) ever more open global trading regime. It was also highly significant that the global management and amelioration of climate change has hitherto been pursued within a United Nations framework and has therefore sat outside the responsibilities of this interconnected set of global governance institutions.

That system can hardly be judged a great success today. Had it performed even the modest task for which it was designed, we would surely not have experienced the financial crisis of 2008–9 and suffered the subsequent Great Recession, and we would not now be witnessing the lack of progress in both the ongoing WTO trade round and the UN climate change talks. Clearly, something is not working – and, put in these terms, it has not been working for a long time. The fact is that the current neoliberal system of global governance is presently locked in a mode of endemic indecision. As we have seen, it was not that ambitious in the first place, but it does not seem any longer that it can strike the deals that are needed to keep even its limited aspirations airborne. The shifting balance of power amongst the leading states in the world has made things just too complex and of itself necessitates the striking of a new deal. In short, we need something better, something more intensive and sophisticated as a system of global governance, something underpinned by a vision of how we want the world to be run, precisely so that citizens in different countries can then decide how they want their political economies to operate on their behalf. The good news is that we know we can have this, because (once more) we have, to some extent at least, had it before – from 1944 to the beginning of the 1970s.

The key global governance institutions that we highlighted earlier – the IMF, the World Bank and the WTO – were all conceived as part of a vision for the restructuring of the post-Second World War order that was enshrined at the famous Bretton Woods Conference of 1944. All of this is of course well known. But what is worth reminding ourselves is that the original vision, and indeed the initial working of the system, was much, much richer in aspiration and in practice than the narrower, more limited, successor to Bretton Woods that came into being during the neoliberal heyday of the 1980s. Within the academic world, this system was famously described by John Ruggie (1982) as a form of 'embedded liberalism', by which he meant that a significant measure of liberalism had been safely and securely grounded within the social and political orders of key participant countries. Within the world of political ideas more generally, it was seen to constitute the underpinning political economy of social democracy.

In a new era characterized by much greater openness and interdependence, we cannot hope to create a new 'Bretton Woods' simply by emulating the form taken by a series of bygone institutions. Many projects and thinkers have tried to do this over many years, and they have all failed. They have mostly tended to look back, rather than forward, which is actually what we now need to do. It *is* possible to begin to design a new package of rules and institutions for better global governance and to infuse that package with a spirit that is akin to that which drove the original Bretton Woods settlement and yet is at the same time firmly post-Bretton Woods in its grasp of changed realities.

In our view, the key question is a straightforward one. What might such a global hosting system for various new models of civic capitalism look like? We think better global governance would have to possess the following four characteristics.

1. It does need a renewed and extended vision. On this front, a great opportunity presents itself. This is the process already under way at the United Nations whereby the former Millennium Development Goals (MDGs) are being reworked for the post-2015 era. Whatever one thinks of the limits and nature of the existing MDGs, they have been hugely influential in setting the tone of global ambition for more than a decade. After all, no fewer than 150 heads of state signed up to the Millennium Declaration in September 2000. We need now to take a step further forward along the lines proposed by Sakiko Fukuda-Parr (2010) who has identified what she describes as 'the missing MDG'. In her view, this should be the goal of seeking to reduce inequality within and between countries. How apt! The post-2015 vision for global

governance should be, genuinely, to 'make globalization more inclusive' (and hence more global).

2. It also requires a coordinating agency to steer the global political economy. Again, because of the panicky move made by President George W. Bush (2008) at the beginning of the global financial crisis – at a time when he is supposed to have observed colloquially that 'this sucker could go down' – a G20 now exists at the level of leaders and heads of government. It has met nine times thus far and by common consent has fallen away in effectiveness and indeed unity following a highly promising start. Yet it is still there and it has the great political advantage of representing, via its twenty member states, some 80–90 per cent of the world's GDP and trade. As such, it has the capacity to steer and to provide the political will and muscle to underpin global governance. Accordingly, we have to work hard to think of ways to improve its current modus operandi.

3. It must be grounded as well within a truly coherent set of global governance institutional pillars, all of which in effect take their political lead from the G20. The particular elements of this structure can be debated and changes in mandate are undoubtedly needed for some current institutions. For all that, the presence on the scene already of the IMF, the World Bank, the WTO and now the Financial Stability Board is a good starting point. It should be remembered that these bodies are seen in US 'tea party' circles as constituting elements of an embryonic and dangerous global state that needs to be brought down. From our perspective, these institutions should be defended and improved. But what does urgently need to be added to the mix is a mechanism that can bring climate change directly into the global policy debate alongside issues of growth, stability and development. It cannot any longer be safely left outside the main tent. If this means creating a new global institution, then so be it.

4. It would finally be greatly facilitated by much more deliberation, debate and argument about global choices and options. In other words, new 'top-down' moves, as above, must be complemented by equally important new 'bottom-up' initiatives. This is really vital and is often neglected – and it is integral, we think, to any project to make the institutions of global governance answer to a civic capitalist agenda. We mean deliberation both with a 'hard edge' (as illustrated, for example, in the debates between state representatives in the UN General Assembly and in the UN system as a whole), but also with a 'soft edge', as manifested in the activism of global civil society, in the global academy of ideas and also, although as yet to an insufficient degree, in the global media. This type of deliberation really does alter the climate of opinion in which 'mega-multilateralism' (Hoffmann 2014) can then do its business.

In sum, we argue that by these various means a reformed and improved system of global governance can both serve as the guiding intelligence of the global political economy *and* reflect to some degree a sense of the global popular will. Importantly, too, it can also function as the incubator for the growth of a host of civic capitalisms. Inside such a world order, they at least have a chance.

Conclusion

In the preceding pages, we have travelled a long distance and covered a lot of ground: from the micro to the macro; from the local to the global; from the capitalism we have to the capitalism we might have; and from the crisis within which we remain mired to the wholesale renewal of our institutions and the ideas which animate them which we see as the key to a sustained and sustainable recovery.

In the process, we have sought to explain the need for a fundamental reform of the untempered Anglo-liberal capitalism whose crisis this is and to make the case for a more profoundly civic capitalism in its stead. Capitalism, we have argued, needs to be made to work for us – not least since the trust that, until recently, we were so happy to place in it has so palpably and poignantly failed to secure the collective public good over the long term. Capitalism, in short, has let us down – and we need to learn from the lessons of that.

We now know what we should probably have realized all along – that capitalism is far from inherently benign just as it is far from inherently self-regulating and self-equilibrating. It needs to be held to account and it needs to be effectively regulated if it is to play its rightful role in securing the collective public good. It needs to be made to serve us ... not us it. What we have sought to show in this essay is that making capitalism work for us is not only both possible and desirable but that, as the crisis shows so well, it is and can be made good for capitalism too. There is no trade-off here as we previously fooled ourselves into believing. Unregulated capitalism does not regulate itself. It is not self-equilibrating and markets do not maximize growth and wealth – the size of the pie, in the familiar analogy – over the long term. Indeed, as we now see all too clearly, they just tend to ensure that, even if the pie grows, it goes off all the sooner – affecting those with the bigger slices just as much as those with less.

Finally, the concept of civic capitalism reminds us that we can be, and indeed have been, slaves to perceived capitalist imperatives – and that this has done us no good, bringing us to the brink of economic and environmental crisis. To resolve either crisis, let alone both, we need to think again – regulating and governing capitalism and capitalist markets for an agreed social purpose. That is what we mean by civic capitalism. The severity of our current plight – domestic and planetary – means that we have to build a new capitalism and we need to do so urgently. This is likely to prove a demanding and a painful process and the transition will be long and arduous. But we have a rare and perhaps a singular opportunity to get this right, a rare choice and the responsibility to future generations which comes with that choice. In the recent past, we entrusted that choice to the markets;

we now need to reclaim it and to take responsibility for it ourselves. The argument applies widely, but to nowhere more forcefully than Britain. Quite simply, the British people and their future leaders need to devise together a design brief for such a civic capitalism. Our aim has been to set out, as we see it, some of the parameters of that debate in order to clarify the nature of the choice that faces us. The legacy will last for generations; at stake in our choice is the economic, institutional and environmental sustainability of our society. We can only hope that we all get it right.

Part II

Engaging Civic Capitalism

The Omission of Real Democracy

Fred Block

In the 1930s, the global economic crisis generated a profusion of radical and revolutionary visions for reconstructing society. Anarchism, communism, socialism and social democracy competed with various forms of fascism and corporatism. In both Europe and North America, those who preferred maintaining the status quo were often a minority. In contrast, the global crisis that began in 2008 has not generated any comparable profusion of radical ideas. Even Thomas Piketty's (2014) recent bestseller limits itself to proposing a global tax on wealth, rather than challenging the structure of ownership or property. The proportions have been reversed: most people seem to want to retain the familiar economic status quo with a few minor reforms, while the advocates of deep restructuring appear to be a tiny minority.

For this reason, the essay by Colin Hay and Anthony Payne on 'civic capitalism' is very much welcome; it begins the process of imagining real alternatives to the economic arrangements that failed so dramatically in 2008. They argue that the 'model of capitalism' that has been in place for the last thirty years in Britain (and in the United States as well) is definitively broken and needs to be replaced. They call for a fundamental shift to an investment-led model of growth that prioritizes protecting the environment from climate change, improving the quality of life and reducing inequalities of income and wealth. They also stress that our existing system for tracking economic output by quarterly changes in GDP is profoundly flawed and has become a major obstacle to the development of bold new policies. The problem is that many of the objectives that they prioritize are simply not included in the GDP calculation. We could, for example, achieve very dramatic reductions in greenhouse gases but, if this came through using energy more efficiently, it might actually appear that GDP was falling.

I am in complete agreement with the priorities that Hay and Payne propose and I think they are also correct to identify our system of economic measurement as a powerful buttress for the global status quo. Nevertheless, I have serious disagreements with them about the labels that they use. They suggest the term 'civic capitalism' for the new model that they favour, but I doubt that this term will work to advance their cause. My objection is not that of a traditional socialist or social democrat who believes that they would be more effective if they were explicitly offering something other than just another flavour of 'capitalism'. In fact, I believe, as I think they do, that terms such as socialism and social democracy have lost whatever meaning they once had and that they are unlikely – anytime soon – to capture the imagination of people seeking a genuine alternative to the current system.

My concern is rather that the word 'capitalism' has come to have powerful connotations that cannot be negated by adding an attractive adjective such as 'civic'. Hay and Payne correctly note that 'we can be, and indeed have been, slaves to perceived capitalist imperatives – and that this has done us no good, bringing us to the brink of economic and environmental crisis'. This is correct, but the problem is that the very word 'capitalism' now incorporates the very imperatives that both these authors and I want to escape. In short, when most people hear the word 'capitalism', it suggests to them an economic system in which disproportionate wealth and power is inevitably concentrated in a small class of extremely wealthy owners. It follows logically that a 'kinder and gentler' capitalism or one with more effective forms of public regulation is not really feasible because those owners will simply pick up their marbles and go home. The endless tax cuts and contractions of the public sector during the last thirty years have been anticipatory concessions to the 'capitalists', just to make sure that they keep the game going with levels of investment and employment that will never be sufficient to put everyone to work.

The point, however, is that these claims about capitalist imperatives are, in fact, false. The historical reality is that profit-oriented economies have worked well in democratic societies precisely because governments impose effective regulations and limits on what businesses do. In fact, when owners have too much political influence, they usually make money through predation, rather than through increasing efficiency. This is precisely why oligarch-dominated societies tend to be economically stagnant; the wealthy just divide up the revenues and give almost no thought to innovation or 'creative destruction'. In fact, almost all of the historical instances of durable and dynamic market economies occurred when there were powerful counterweights to the influence of big business.

So why is this belief so widespread that a profit-oriented system only works when everybody lets the owners have their way on such issues as taxation, regulation and employee rights? Well, this is precisely the line that Friedrich Hayek, Milton Friedman and their many market fundamentalist followers have been pushing for the last seven decades. In their idealized and utopian vision of how a market economy works, all that firms have to do is respond to the signals of the price system. By definition, taxes, regulations and employee rights will only distort those signals and those distortions make everybody worse off. So the only way to assure the optimal use of resources is to leave owners alone to maximize their profits.

This is, of course, completely wrong; there is no such thing as a functioning market without government imposing rules and regulations. But when a lie is repeated as endlessly as this one, it gains traction. So lots of people believe: (1) that capitalism is a system of profit-oriented firms competing in a competitive market; (2) that the market system works best when government is small and minimizes its economic role; so it follows that (3) profit-oriented firms need to get their way if the economic system is to be productive. For people who accept this syllogism, 'civic capitalism' is dead on arrival.

The further irony is that many critics of the existing system also embrace this syllogism as a way to persuade people that we need a radically different social order. In Europe and North America, people on the left often argue explicitly or believe in their hearts that the only way that working-class and poor people can ever regain the prosperity of the 'golden age' between 1945 and 1975 is through a transition to socialism. And since most of these people also recognize the improbability of such a transition any time soon, they end up believing that resistance to the next round of retrenchment is probably futile. In short, this particular syllogism has empowered the right and disempowered the left. By inserting the pleasant word 'civic', Hay and Payne have done nothing to alter this dynamic.

But there is a word that has the potential to break this impasse if it is properly explained, and it is a very old word indeed: namely, 'democracy'. The explanation involves three basic steps. The first is that the historical movement to create 'government of the people, by the people, and for the people' has been the single most important factor in generating dynamic economic growth that raises the standard of living of most people. The connection between democratization and economic growth works through two main channels. First, electoral democracy, combined with political and civil rights, allows people to mobilize to block predation by economic elites; through government regulations, businesses are literally forced to focus on the more efficient production of things that people actually want, while also limiting 'public bads', such as environmental degradation. Second, through democratic channels, people are able to gain access to key resources such as better education, better health care and greater economic security, all of which enhance their capabilities as employees and citizens. In a word, effective democratic governance produces positive economic consequences.

But the second step of the argument is the critical one. The process of democratizing society is like riding a bike; it is stable only when it is constantly moving forward. Historically, this has had two major dimensions. The first has been the extension of full democratic participation, including suffrage and political and civil rights, to an ever larger share of the population. The second has been the process of deepening democracy by creating new participatory institutions and extending the people's voice into key economic decisions. The 1960s New Left pushed on both of these dimensions, but its calls for economic democracy, participatory democracy, or 'autogestion', were rejected.

But the architects of the Reagan–Thatcher reaction to the 1960s were not content to stop further democratization; they sought to push it into reverse by reasserting the necessary dominance of 'the market'. From the crushing of trade unions to the privatization of public services to the autonomy of central banks, democratic processes were systematically undermined. Democratic governance was redefined in Schumpeterian terms as the opportunity for people occasionally to choose the elites that would maintain their continued subordination. The results have been unsurprising; as democracy became an increasingly empty slogan, the economy ceased to work for all but the top 1 per cent.

The third step should now be obvious. What we want and need is not 'civic capitalism'; it is Real Democracy. Real Democracy is both the means that we use and the end that we seek. By resuming the interrupted process of democratizing society, we increase dramatically the odds of achieving sustainable prosperity. Moreover, Real Democracy is also the solution to the profound distrust of politics and of the entire political class that is now endemic to most of the developed market societies.

The project of Real Democracy incorporates the key elements of the Hay–Payne economic programme, but it also emphasizes the element of democratic reform at all levels of government. This means, as the authors argue, reforming the institutions of global economic governance and making them far more responsive to the bottom-up initiatives of global civil society. It also requires dismantling the various restrictions imposed at the national and European Community levels that interfere with popular sovereignty, such as the arbitrary spending limits imposed by Maastricht or the control of credit creation by autonomous central banks. Most vitally, it involves bringing meaningful democratic participation to government at the local, metropolitan and regional levels, to the workplace and to the realm of finance (Block 2014).

The logic behind this democratization process is that it is no longer reasonable to imagine that localities can rely on big corporations to create either needed employment opportunities or sustainable growth. Rather, prosperity will depend on investments in infrastructure and bottom-up efforts to revitalize local economies through improved services, third-sector jobs and new business creation. But it makes no sense to leave the decisions over infrastructure and what activities will be financed in the hands of either public or private technocrats. Rather, we need to create new mechanisms through which people can collectively participate in these decisions that will shape how their communities will develop over time. Moreover, the resulting revitalization of local democratic governance will, in turn, help to strengthen parliamentary democracy as citizens gain a deeper knowledge of what is at stake in national-level decisions.

To be sure, what I am calling Real Democracy is not a bumper sticker for the next election; it is a project that will take generations. But using this language has, I think, two major advantages that Hay and Payne would be wise to consider. First, the binary of socialism vs capitalism (even if it is relabelled as 'civic capitalism') has become a theoretical prison that keeps us from thinking rationally about key issues of political economy. Second, democratization has been the most powerful emancipatory force at work in the world for the last 250 years. As we know from the Squares of Tiananmen and Tahrir and many other defeats, its progress has been painfully uneven and incomplete and monarchs have frequently been superseded by oligarchs with even greater wealth. Nevertheless, a project of social and economic renewal that does not tap into these widely shared democratic aspirations has little chance of success.

The Next Steps

Colin Crouch

The continuing global dominance of neoliberalism as a political ideology is by no means unchallenged. Across a wide range of issues, from financial services to the health risks of many processed food products, politicians of all parties have to make repeated responses to public concern. Even if these responses are more often than not public relations exercises rather than substantive action, governments are rarely able to give the public the official neoliberal answer: that the market will respond adequately to all problems. Further, in many countries inequality has become an issue in a way that has not been the case for decades. Attacks on the welfare state mainly have to rely on scare stories about benefits scroungers; outside the United States, it is far less easy for neoliberals to launch frontal assaults on the idea of social citizenship itself. Indeed, very rarely does neoliberalism appear as a proud ideology in its own right, dominating the appeal of a major political party. It always appears alongside, or perhaps even hiding behind, other broad appeals that exist in only uneasy if not downright contradictory coalitions with neoliberalism itself. Usually, these are conservative, traditional, sometimes even xenophobic appeals; sometimes social democratic ones. It is not at the level of open, democratic politics that neoliberalism exercises its main power.

Rather, it works at the level of post-democratic elite politics, through the activities of corporate lobbyists, seeking either freedom from regulation, contracts for the delivery of privatized public services, bank bailouts or political favours. Here, just as much as in the democratic arena, neoliberalism finds itself caught in contradictions: for, while theoretically it is an ideology of free markets, in reality it is about corporate political privilege, which should be anathema to true neoliberals. Actually existing neoliberalism, which is the politico-economic phenomenon with which we have to deal in real life, rather than that of economics textbooks, is often a 'socialism of the rich'.

Neoliberalism is protected from the vulnerability of its position precisely through those linkages between the corporate and political worlds. While these crude facts of power remain formidable obstacles to the practical realization of alternatives, they cannot disguise the fact that, at the level of theory, ideology and popular appeal, neoliberalism is a soft target. Politicians and think-tanks of most political orientations are in thrall to it, but the task of providing them with coherent alternatives is not in itself daunting. It has become a bored cliché of media discussion that the left has come up with no alternatives to neoliberalism, but this reflects only the idleness of the commentators. In reality, there has been a plethora of discussion of alternative economic and social policy strategies. It might be argued that these have been heterogeneous, lacking the overall integration of neoliberalism. This complaint overlooks the contradictions that beset neoliberalism itself, but also overlooks some emerging consensus about alternatives.

Much of this consensus is embodied in Hay and Payne's development of the idea of civic capitalism. This captures continued commitment to a capitalist, rather than a state-owned, economy, which is an important starting point for alternatives that wish to avoid being lured back into the chimera of a state-controlled or vaguely defined popularly controlled economy. And 'civic' is a welcome reformulation of the basic idea of common or public goods that forms an essential base to the critique of an economy dominated by markets and corporate power alone.

Hay and Payne here capture the crucial point that day-to-day politics so studiously ignores: modern western society has extraordinary collective needs and interdependencies. Climate change and other environmental problems, many of them products of our way of life, are threatening that way of life itself unless we can come together to find solutions. Further, our economies and societies are increasingly interdependent, bound together as we are through the globalized exchanges of goods, services and financial flows. These interdependencies appear as competitive national rivalries, but in trade the continued success of any one human group is usually improved by the success of everyone else. The authors escape the parochial nationalism of standard political debate in fully appreciating the indispensability of cross-national collaboration to tackle most of these issues. They also understand that sophisticated economies also need advanced infrastructures – transport and communications networks, resources of skilled labour, shared regulatory standards – that depend on collective effort. Western societies are also (in general) rich and can afford to do something about these collective issues while also leaving the great majority of individuals with well-provided private lives. But these societies are also becoming increasingly unequal, decreasingly willing to produce public goods or cover collective risks, while the products of increasing wealth reward an ever smaller minority.

These realities mean that social democracy, revivified through the concept of the social investment welfare state and in alliance with green movements, stands as the most likely political vehicle for the approach that Hay and Payne outline. I see just three questions that they leave incomplete and that remain for the next stage of the debate.

The Problem of the European Union

First, as has become standard with virtually all British contributions to these issues, they ignore the existence of the European Union, or perhaps just assume that Britain will soon cease to be a member of it. Today, the EU plays a paradoxical part in attempts to frame alternatives to neoliberalism. On the one hand, it stands as a primary agent of neoliberal strategies, especially in the encroachments of competition policy on the terrains of social policy and labour markets. On the other hand, it is difficult to see how nationstates of the size of even the largest European countries can expect to play the major role at the international level that Hay and Payne recognize to be so important without working together through the EU. Despite the neoliberal stance of most current EU policy, despite their diversity, the states of western (though not central and eastern) Europe remain closer to civic capitalism than do the United States, Japan or other advanced capitalist economies (Crouch forthcoming). Whether or not Britain remains a member of the Union, it will be through the efforts of left-of-centre political forces within it that the best chance of contesting global neoliberalism will come.

A major example of what I mean is the strategy for a social investment welfare state that has been developed by social policy specialists across a range of western European countries, but of which Hay and Payne make no mention (Hemerijck 2012; Morel, Palier and Palme 2012; Vandenbroucke, Hemerijck and Palier 2011). It contests the idea of welfare spending as just a drain on national economies, pointing out the role of many areas of social spending, such as education, childcare and unemployment support, in strengthening economies. The analysis not only identifies priority areas for spending but also provides a basis for criticism of some other kinds, such as early retirement schemes. Hay and Payne certainly share much of this substantive agenda, and I fully support their case for not limiting social objectives to economic ones. (For example, they make a fine point in stressing that education has value as imparting a sense of social empowerment, which reaches well beyond current preoccupations with the possible contribution of education to increasing GDP.) However, the social investment welfare state provides a valuable focus for asserting the positive role of social policy, and it would contribute to the overall thrust of the authors' case. This is more an example of the isolation of British political thinking from what is going on elsewhere in western Europe than a real divergence of policy.

The Problem of the State

Next comes a more difficult problem of the role of the state. Hay and Payne see its centrality as the agency for representing public and collective interests against private ones. They are right in this. Attempts to show that the market can replace the state in its care for the commons have been shown to be false, whether theoretically in the economic analysis of externalities or in practice in such issues as the environmental crisis. In general, to denigrate the role of the state is to deny the existence of any shared or public interests at all.

There are, however, two problems with this traditional approach: it ignores the corruption of the state; and it overlooks the role of other, admittedly small, means of protecting the collective.

The former problem is the other side of the coin of the corruption of pure market neoliberalism by the reality of corporate lobbying. By bringing economic power to bear in the polity, the political role of corporate wealth undermines market and state alike. How can we trust the state to defend collective and public goods when the main interests operating on states, supplying them with advice, seconding staff to them through the revolving door, funding party campaigns, are the very corporations whose activities need to be regulated in the public good? The weakness of much regulatory policy that Hay and Payne describe so well stems primarily from this source. As society becomes more unequal, so the wealthy, embedded in corporate influence, acquire even more political power, which in turn is used to promote policies that enhance their wealth. It is a vicious spiral that leads the state increasingly to become a corporate wolf in a public-goods sheep's clothing.

Just as we need the EU but cannot trust it in its present political form, so we both need and cannot trust the state. We need constant vigilance by informed citizens, criticizing, monitoring, whistle-blowing, laying bare, campaigning. And this links with my second problem with the role of the state: the existence of other forces working for public goods, classically described by Elinor Ostrom (1990). These can be found in many places, from charities, to those precious public institutions that are state-funded but operate at more than arm's length from the government of the day, even to some philanthropic activities of the wealthy and some cor-porations. They lack the formal legitimacy of the state as guardian of a public interest, and this must always be remembered; but they contribute to the de facto pluralism of public life. Also – and here is the link to the former point – they are often the base for the criticizing, whistle-blowing and so on that we need to supplement formal democracy in coping with a state under strong pressure from corporate power. Reassertion of the centrality of the state must also deal with responding to its frequent failure.

The Problem of Class

Finally, there is the problem of the social base for a critique of corporate neoliberalism, following the decline of the organized manual working class of industrial society. If the problem of confronting neoliberalism is primarily one of power rather than ideas, this cannot be neglected. I wrote in *Post-Democracy* (Crouch 2004) that the middle and lower occupational groups of post-industrial society lack the capacity to generate a critical political consciousness, so disparate are their living conditions. However, I missed a potential answer to this puzzle in another part of my own discussion.

I mentioned the feminist movement, along with environmentalism, as a phenomenon that had been able to challenge the limits of post-democratic political debate. I failed to notice the obvious point that a clear majority of occupants of those middle and junior post-industrial sectors are women (but see Crouch 2013: ch. 9).

Working women are well equipped to be the carriers of a constructive challenge to neoliberal hegemony. Most simply, they are not a minority. Further, although they long ago acquired political citizenship, they still suffer from a range of gender-based disadvantages in participating fully in life outside the home. Their identity therefore has a powerful political dimension. The fact that several of these disadvantages have been addressed in many countries in recent years does not weaken the force of this. History has frequently shown us that disadvantaged groups are most likely to press for change when they see some signs of improvement. Third, women constitute the majority of people working in middle and lower positions in the services sectors of the economy, the very social location to which one must look for any new challenge to dominance by elites (Oesch 2006).

Finally, and more difficult to demonstrate than these three points, women are, by both the long-term and the recent distinctive history of the lives of a large majority of them, better equipped than the majority of men to resist the central thrust of the neoliberal project and stand for public goods. The potentiality of this has been concealed by the fact that until now most successful policies for women's advance have had a shared neoliberal and social democratic agenda, against gradually shrinking conservative opposition, for liberation from various constraints imposed by past law and custom. Except when it comes to demands for state support of child care, neoliberals have no problems with this. But deeper issues lie behind women's continued advance. Neoliberalism requires of members of society, if they are to avoid failure, a single-minded devotion to maximizing interests that are defined according to a strict economic calculus. Areas of life that lie outside the scope of that approach are either to be ignored or forced to be redefined so that they can take their place within that calculus. I do not believe that many people of either gender can accept this over the long haul; but men are more likely to adapt to it. The dual role that women usually play in contemporary society, balancing work and home, places them at the sharp end of these struggles. If gender relations become more balanced, then an increasing number of men will become like this too. A convergence on a hitherto predominately female life is important to a politics defined by women but benefiting many men too, which is necessary if feminism is to play this more general role.

Some aspects of this are readily understandable and turned into familiar political demands. For example, we need a politicization of the problem of work/life balance, talked about by very many people but not by political parties (McGinnity and Russell 2013). But there are deeper aspects that will become more pressing as the neoliberal strategy itself has more victories. For example, as Philip Mirowski (2013) has demonstrated, the marketization of everything eventually requires a fragmentation of the self. In a highly flexible neoliberal economy where eventually all support for the unemployed will have been withdrawn, people need to be repeatedly re-presenting and redefining themselves to be attractive to employers' constantly changing requirements. This is especially true in the personal services sectors (where women predominate), where the self becomes part of the product. To present oneself effectively against a constantly shifting set of criteria requires constant attention to the signals one gives out through one's entire lifestyle – and therefore through one's life as a consumer as, in a fully marketed society, there is little outside the realm of purchase and consumption. This takes us into the deepest issue raised by Hay and Payne: the need for public life to be about something more than maximizing a narrowly defined economic growth.

In Search of an Alternative

Andrew Gamble

One of the starting points for Colin Hay and Anthony Payne's essay on civic capitalism is the urgent need to start thinking about alternatives. Six years after the greatest financial turbulence since the 1930s, there is still no clear sign of any alternative emerging to the present dispensation. There is a ferment of radical new ideas but not much sign yet of radical policy initiatives or new radical movements. We are at present stuck with the old policy paradigm. Its familiar common sense is still being paraded day after day as though the events of 2007 and 2008 never happened. Banks are still paying bonuses and inequality remains as pronounced as ever. Some people long for a new Keynes to shine a light on our problems and guide us to a new way of ordering our affairs. But so far no new Keynes has come. There have been some major intellectual interventions, like Thomas Piketty's book *Capital in the Twenty-First Century*, which have had significant impact (Piketty 2014). Everyone is talking about inequality now, and there is widespread concern over what the continuance of the trends of the last thirty years means for capitalism and for democracy. Yet, despite Piketty's intellectual success, there are still few signs that governments anywhere are intending to do much about the rising tide of inequality or even know where to begin. There is a resignation and fatalism which is hard to shake. It was briefly ruffled by the Occupy Movement, which attracted considerable publicity in 2011 and 2012 and coined a memorable slogan: 'We are the 99 per cent.' But more recently it has not been able to maintain momentum.

We need to understand why many of the ideas seemingly discredited by the extraordinary events of 2007–8 remain so resilient and the policies which they legitimate so powerful in our world (Schmidt and Thatcher 2013). But we also need to understand the potential for change and what we might do to help bring it about. We are living through a period of profound economic and political restructuring of our political economy, and this is bound to yield many opportunities for positive changes. But it is characteristic of such periods that they can also be profoundly discouraging. We should remember that the great convulsion of the 1930s was a period of huge ideological and political confusion. The collapse of the gold standard and the international trading system, and its reorganization into relatively closed currency and commercial and ultimately military blocs, was on a scale much greater than anything we have witnessed, in part because this time around leading governments have done everything they can to avert a complete financial meltdown and economic collapse. But even though the change in the 1930s was so profound and so visible, the political responses were very mixed. There was a widespread feeling that the old liberal international order was finished and that the future lay with forms of national protectionism and organized capitalism. Even Keynes advocated protectionism for a while (Keynes 1933). But there was no simple formula – instead, a wide variety of experiments. They included the National Socialist regime in Germany, the New Deal in the United States, the beginnings of social democracy in Sweden and Conservative corporatism in Britain. Some of these political experiments were progressive, but the majority were not. They were defensive reactions to an increasingly hostile world. The political balance swung firmly to the right and towards dictatorship in many parts of the world. Both economic *and* political liberalism were discredited.

What is sometimes forgotten about the 1930s is that Keynes did not write his *General Theory* until 1936, eight years after the Great Crash of 1929, and the ideas within it did not really begin to shape policy until the 1940s. It needed a world war and the huge restructuring of relations within and between states which this generated to create a new international liberal order and the flowering of Keynesianism and embedded liberalism. It became possible to interpret the outcome of the convulsions of the first half of the twentieth century as laying the foundations for a new progressive dispensation, but it did not seem a likely outcome in the 1930s, and there was no guarantee that it would happen. What made it actually happen was not just Keynes but a host of other intellectual initiatives and political projects, including planning, welfare, world order and the social market of the Ordoliberals. It also required not just military victory for the liberal capitalist states in alliance with the Soviet Union against fascism, but the formation of domestic coalitions capable of formulating and carrying through programmes of domestic reform.

The situation we face today is very different. First of all, there has been no breakdown in the international liberal order. The United States is under greater challenge, but it retains its dominant position. As Hay and Payne argue, it made some concessions in the immediate aftermath of the crisis by giving a much higher profile to the G20 and by altering some of the voting weights in the IMF. But the momentum of change has slowed and the United States currently shows little ambition to remodel the system of international global governance which it has presided over for seventy years. Large and potentially transformative shifts are taking place in the international economy, with the rise of China, India and Brazil, as well as many other new powers. But this has not yet reached the point where the United States is being directly challenged or feels the need to make major concessions or give up any of the 'exorbitant privileges' it has enjoyed for so long (Eichengreen 2012). For as long as this is the case, the need for radical changes to the way things are done is likely to be resisted. After the United States reorganized the international liberal order following the turbulence of the 1970s, the embedded liberalism of the Bretton Woods era became much less pronounced, but social democratic regimes still survived and found ways to prosper. The present crisis calls into question whether these will be viable in future, and whether neoliberal logic will be applied ever more rigorously. In response, 'Civic Capitalism' sets out an ambitious programme for creating once again a new progressive model of capitalism. However, it will require underpinning by a new set of international rules if it is to succeed.

There are two obstacles in the way. The first, as already suggested, is the United States, which shows no sign of being willing to accommodate the kind of changes in international rules which would be needed for experiments in civic capitalism to succeed. The second is that civic capitalism is likely to appeal most to those European states which have already established some form of social democracy. The capitalist models which are currently most vibrant, however, are some of the former communist eastern European states and the rising powers. It is not obvious that either group will be much interested in the foreseeable future in the civic capitalist model, and opponents of the civic capitalist model continually point to the increasing competition from the new economies to urge the dismantling of social protection and universalist welfare. Civic capitalism is an immensely attractive idea, and Hay and Payne have skilfully drawn together a wealth of detail showing how it forms an interconnected whole and a plausible model for a new political economy. But its supporters are currently on the defensive because after the crash the world is more, not less, hostile to the kind of initiatives which civic capitalism requires. There are many voices warning about the global race and purporting to show how western prosperity is imperilled by the rise of the East. The slashing of social spending which competitors do not have to bear becomes politically attractive. The global race becomes a race to the bottom.

The importance of what Hay and Payne have done is to show that civic capitalism does constitute a real alternative to this path. They show that what is needed is not just new rules for global governance or a new growth model or new priority on protection against environmental risk, but *all of these*. This requires a politics of great skill since it must operate on many different levels, building local, national and transnational coalitions to make possible the achievement of these goals. Here again, there are some obvious differences from the 1930s. Labour as an organized interest in the capitalist democracies was at that time a powerful component of progressive coalitions. It is a much weaker component today, and the effects of individualization and financialization have made it harder to assert the common interest in civic capitalism. An example of this can be found in attitudes to inequality. Many countries used to support much tighter controls on the degree of inequality permitted. But these have been substantially eroded since the 1970s. The recent example of Radamel Falcao's transfer to Manchester United at a reported wage of £300,000 per week is typical of the huge rates top athletes, bankers and celebrities can now command. But there is little public backlash against such excesses, even in a time of austerity and falling real wages for the majority. Robert Nozick's analysis of why sports fans were happy that major stars, like Wilt Chamberlain, or today Falcao, received such huge financial rewards pinpoints an important aspect of market culture (Nozick 1974).

Although it is easy to see the obstacles to civic capitalism, this does not mean that these cannot be overcome. Ideas often have to incubate a long time before the moment when they can be successfully applied. Neoliberals learnt this from the Fabians (Cockett 1994), and we should learn it anew from the neoliberals. The cogency of these ideas makes this an exciting time for centre-left thinking. They form an essential ingredient in helping to build the political coalitions and identify the political interests which can turn this into a successful political programme. The future events which will make or break such programmes cannot be foreseen. What is certain is that the crisis which began in 2007–8 is far from resolved. It has been contained, but the underlying causes have not gone away (Gamble 2014; Streeck 2014). If these underlying causes are not tackled, there will be further shocks in the future, which might take the form of a financial collapse in China, or a collapse of confidence in the dollar.

Hay and Payne rightly emphasize two pressing problems which signal the importance of moving in the direction they suggest. The first is productivity, and the increasing difficulty of western economies to raise their productivity fast enough to support rising real wages. Unless this change can be reversed, the outlook for liberal capitalism is bleak since personal debt cannot grow exponentially to support the lifestyles western consumers have come to expect. This stagnation of incomes for the majority is a huge unresolved issue which has profound political implications. It is closely related to the deflation trap into which the neoliberal order has plunged. Preventing the deflationary bias in this system has become the preoccupation of the monetary authorities, but it is not clear that they know how to overcome it within the present parameters, as the recent setbacks of 'Abenomics' in Japan seem to demonstrate. The second problem is climate change. As the evidence for its effects grows, this will have a profound effect on how we think about our present political economy, changing our attitudes towards growth and well-being. What kinds of growth are sustainable with a viable ecosphere, and what kinds of investments we should be making, and what kinds of restrictions we should be placing on certain kinds of economic activities – all this is likely to start looming much larger in the decades ahead (Gough 2011). The great virtue of the civic capitalism approach is that it puts the emphasis on finding new ways to cooperate between citizens and between nations which can start to tackle some of the problems and the opportunities which liberal capitalism constantly creates. Joseph Schumpeter called it creative destruction. We need to find the will and the wit to tame the destruction and enhance the creativity. Presenting a plausible model of a different kind of capitalism and the sort of policies which might implement it is a good place to start.

'If I Were You, I Wouldn't Start from Here'

*Ian Gough**

'Civic Capitalism' (CC) is the latest of several alternative left-of-centre strategies to explain, cope with and move beyond the present crisis state of capitalism. Since the financial crisis, these have included the Green New Deal (New Economics Foundation 2008), Plan B (Reed and Lawson 2011), the CRESC perspective (Engelen et al. 2011) and the Kilburn Manifesto (Hall, Massey and Rustin 2014), among others. Of course, there have been earlier diagnoses and alternatives; 'Civic Capitalism' reminds me of David Marquand's *The Unprincipled Society* (1988).

Despite significant differences and disagreements, there is a remarkable degree of consensus on several dimensions, including at least the following:

- The 'economy' should be re-embedded in broader society.
- The state should play a leading role in this process.
- Egregious inequality must be directly addressed.
- The financialization of capital must be curbed and regulated.

* Many thanks to Anna Coote and Graham Room for helpful comments on an earlier draft. The usual disclaimer applies.

- Productive and reproductive investment should be expanded.
- Sustainability should form a core goal for economic and social policy.
- New indicators of well-being are urged to replace GDP.
- New forms of democracy and politics need fostering.
- All of this requires an alternative moral dimension to that of neoliberalism.

There is less consensus on some other aspects:

- Is the goal to moderate capitalism (to aim for 'capitalism with an adjective') or to recognize and transit beyond its systemic limits? 'Civic Capitalism' is quite explicit here: 'making capitalism work for us is ... both possible and desirable.'
- How are climate change and environmental threats integrated into the accounts? CC addresses this in some detail.
- To what extent is the role of gendered, unwaged labour and social reproduction recognized as both a critical economic feature and a distinct normative perspective (Fraser 2014)? CC is silent here.
- What are the class and social movements which might challenge neoliberalism? CC is silent here.
- Is the strategy aimed at Britain (thus recognizing the peculiarities of British capitalism), the European Union, the OECD world, or indeed the globe (requiring some recognition that the centre of gravity is shifting to Asia and that in many parts of the world capitalism shows no signs of crisis)? Although written from a British perspective, CC recognizes and briefly addresses some European and global issues.

In this brief reply, I will concentrate on three issues only. First, how can these strategies for coping with capitalist crisis be linked with those required to avert the fast-looming environmental crisis? Second, if slower growth or zero growth is required to achieve environmental sustainability, what does this portend for economic and political strategy? Third, has the neoliberal revolution gone too far, blocking any conceivable social forces that could reverse direction (the 'I wouldn't start from here' problem, as identified by the apocryphal Irishman asked the way to Dublin)?

The Environmental Crisis

To achieve a fifty-fifty chance of avoiding global warming exceeding 2°C by the end of the century, and taking population growth into account, global emissions must be cut from around 7 tonnes CO_2eq per person per year now to no more than 2 by 2050 – a revolutionary downshift of 3.5 times. But, if output per person continues to grow at its present rate (roughly trebling by 2050), then global emissions per unit of output must fall by a factor of 9–10 by 2050 – now only 34 years away. (And remember, an even chance is like playing Russian roulette.)

The dominant strategy for achieving this within a capitalist global order goes by various labels, including 'ecological modernization', 'green growth' and a 'new industrial revolution'. ('Sustainable development' is somewhat different because development does not necessarily entail growth.) CC endorses this approach and provides data and argument showing the unsustainability of the contemporary economic model.

There are three broad mechanisms which can conceivably achieve this revolution. The first, and the most amenable to those neoliberal ideologists who accept the climate science (many do not), is to price carbon so as to impose costs on polluters and thus internalize the externalities they generate, and provide price incentives for sustainable energy. Although this will have a role to play, it is by now clear that it cannot be anywhere near sufficient (and it would have regressive distributive effects to add to the ballooning inequality of past decades). The second alternative, advocated by Lord Stern among others, is to foster a transformative technological/

industrial revolution to decarbonize almost all energy by 2050. The third is to shift the behaviours of consumers in order drastically to save energy and switch to low-carbon consumption.

What is evident is that all three policy responses are required (Grubb, Hourcade and Neuhoff 2013). Moreover, the state must play a big role in all three: setting energy and other prices via taxation and subsidies; regulating standards across a wide spectrum of economic activities; undertaking strategic planning; developing national investment frameworks covering energy, transport, housing and urban forms, electronic networks, climate adaptation and ecosystem maintenance (and not forgetting the whole range of social investment in health, education, training, etc.); the list goes on.

CC adumbrates such a neo-Keynesian strategy of 'sustainable development through investment'; the idea of the state as 'collective goods provider of last resort' summarizes this well. CC also joins a chorus of voices advocating an alternative measure of progress to GDP – in this case a Sustainable Economic Development index. The proposal to create a hybrid GDP-SED index with the weights gradually shifting from the former to the latter over, say, twenty years is original and important.

The Growth Issue

However, CC is adamant that all this does not mean the abandonment of the search for growth – 'quite the contrary'. It is useful to distinguish two perspectives here.

First, it is highly likely that growth, especially in Europe, *will* be slower over the next three decades than over the last three for several reasons: demographic shifts, notable population ageing; the continued, if slower, expansion of the services sector with low or zero productivity growth; rising inequality which stunts demand; and the huge overhang of personal debt. If big carbon mitigation programmes are factored in, then a recent model predicts a further fall in growth rates over the next two decades, as carbon pricing drives up production costs and slows down increases in purchasing power (Demailly et al. 2013). Even if driven by a new green industrial revolution, we should not assume a growth rate in the West of 2 per cent per annum as in the past – perhaps 1 per cent per annum is more likely. This has negative implications for inequality, as Piketty (2014) shows, and for social justice. The post-war welfare state was built on a post-war growth state; its ending would pose radical new issues.

But, second, the argument of ecological economists such as Tim Jackson is that we cannot grow for ever – or indeed, in the rich North, from now on. The argument often advanced that a 'weightless', creative, caring, service-based economy can tread with a light ecological footprint ignores the fact that creative and caring workers will also want to consume a wide range of material goods (Jackson 2009). The hidden assumption is that Britain will continue to import many consumer goods and thus export their emissions. So we must find a progressive way to harmonize slower/stationary growth with both rising well-being and responsible husbandry of the planet. At this point, the strategy of sustainable development through investment is insufficient. In my view, the following strategies and policies then need to play a central role.

First, a strategy for *consumption* should prioritize need satisfiers over want satisfiers, non-material satisfiers over material satisfiers, and low-carbon satisfiers over carbon-intensive satisfiers. (Satisfiers include both goods and services, but also activities and relationships.) There are various ways of doing this, but all mean challenging the enthronement of 'consumer sovereignty', which is very often big-producer and ad-agency sovereignty (Gough 2014). This could be done via taxation of high-carbon luxuries, the public provision of basic-need satisfiers, like energy and water, and a form of carbon allowances and trading, with two separate currencies – money and carbon – for a range of items, including domestic energy, petrol and air travel.

Second, a strategy for *production* could include moving to a shorter working week. Assuming economy-wide productivity continues to rise (if not at past rates), this amounts to taking more of these gains in the form of rising 'leisure', rather than consumption. Since 1975, when they had similar hours of work, the United States has reduced average hours by 4 per cent and Germany by 22 per cent (Schor 2012). All other things being equal, Germany has deployed its productivity dividend in a less environmentally harmful way than the United States. Several European countries have initiated experiments in reducing work-time which offer constructive lessons, but the current grain of British and EU social policy – the social investment state – is the complete opposite: getting more people into work and into full-time work and fetishizing 'hard-working families'.

Third, a new strategy for the *welfare state* would be needed to cope with some side effects of environmental programmes, as well as to build capacities, meet unmet needs and tackle egregious inequality. This certainly means building an alternative to 'austerity' as a macro-policy, but it requires more: a new emphasis on prevention as the social policy approach of first choice and building on the uncommodified household and civic economies to establish a default strategy of 'co-production' in the welfare services. These measures would complement the necessary taxation and redistribution of wealth and unearned incomes.

Finally, an emphasis on localism would be a new priority in the most centralized nation in the developed world – namely, Britain. This would need to extend to finance, planning and investment, as well as social policy. But, more radically, it would support the 'foundational economy', that part of the private sector producing a range of necessities – telecoms, supermarkets, retail banks – which is also relatively sheltered from foreign competition (Bowman et al. 2014). Such a localist strategy would begin to cut down on food miles and other carbon-extravagant practices, as well as reducing exposure to trade shocks.

None of these proposals – apart from the fourth to a limited extent – figures in 'Civic Capitalism' or in most alternative strategies. I would want to see these worked into a transitional strategy for eco-social policy, starting from an assumption of low economic growth and working up to a scenario of deliberately limited growth.

The Strange Non-Death of Neoliberalism

But this brings us back to where we are now, summarized in the title of Colin Crouch's book (2011). Both a sustainable growth economy and a sustainable zero-growth economy would require extensive state intervention. Yet to advocate such an expanded role for the state without addressing the deep embeddedness of neoliberal capitalism is misleading. Finance capital pursues the shortest of short-term advantage; powerful corporate and financial actors lobby governments and subvert democratic demands; the capacities of states have been denuded over three decades and their dependence on debt and bond markets extended. In short, we must evaluate economic policies, such as those we are addressing, in full knowledge of the world in which we operate. This induces great pessimism that the near-decarbonization of global energy systems can remotely be achieved – let alone within 34 years.

Yet capitalism cannot exist in a free-floating form; it requires countervailing social institutions to moderate its worst excesses. This has been argued from different theoretical directions – Marxist: the absolute exploitation of labourers and the degraded reproduction of labour power, countered with the campaign for the 10-hour working day and numerous subsequent state welfare policies (Gough 1979); Polanyian: the excessive commodification of the fictitious commodities of Labour, Land and Money fosters a triple crisis (Streeck 2014b); and Feminist: the labour process is founded on the social reproduction activities of women and families (Fraser 2014).

All this is well known, and was enshrined in the mixed economies and welfare states of the post-war – and Cold War – period that marked the heyday of democratic capitalism. But functionality does not drive countervailing action;

collective agency is necessary. Over the last three decades, the pursuit of 'legitimate greed' by capital owners has reversed these gains and brought about the problems which these strategies intend to address. The problem, as Streeck is the latest to argue, is that the neoliberal economic order has gradually weakened all democratic constraints on the economy. This has been caused partly by the emasculation of trades unions and 'democratic class struggle' and their replacement with 'market-conforming democracy'; and partly by the commodification and marketization of almost all the myriad social institutions that previously constrained the pursuit of profit.

In Streeck's (2014b) words, the *Staatsvolk* of citizens has been disempowered and the *Marktvolk* of bondholders now rules states. This feeds into citizen apathy and a further weakening of alternatives to the status quo. Thus all the normal restraints over capitalist greed have been removed or weakened. That only leaves 'far-sighted elites' (such as, for example, Adair Turner in Britain), but in a final twist these elites gradually become globalized and de-linked from the interests of any particular nation-state.

This is the economic-social-political order that is now called on to tackle the urgent and egregious challenge of climate change and pursue the twin goals of planetary sustainability and human well-being. As has been said, 'if I were you, I wouldn't start from here'.

Putting the 'Civic' More into the Mix

Gavin Kelly with Conor D'Arcy

In seeking to convey the overall flavour of their sweeping and synoptic project, Hay and Payne gave it a clear banner heading: civic capitalism. As the authors say, labels matter. They did not opt for 'regulated', 'inclusive' or 'strategic' capitalism, though arguably each of these might have sat just as comfortably with the thrust of their overall argument. Instead they chose 'civic' – to be understood, in their words, in its simplest and most straightforward sense: relating to and utilized on behalf of all citizens. The recent history of the term underlines the variety of interpretations which fall under it and the uses to which it can be put. In this brief response, we set out a few thoughts prompted by this label and the territory it could cover. In doing so, we raise some questions about, and possible further directions for, their project.

Hay and Payne are not the first to invoke the prefix 'civic' to signal a new line of political argument. In the early 1990s, there was something of a competitive struggle to appropriate the prefix. The notion of civic conservatism gained currency on the British centre-right, not least due to the work of David Willetts (1994), who sought to refresh Oakeshottian conservatism, later fusing it with game theory, in order to mount a contemporary argument for placing the relationship between free markets and civil society at the heart of politics. At around the same time several thinkers on the centre-left, particularly in the United States, developed the notion of 'civic liberalism' – an attempt to popularize Michael Walzer's contention that part of the purpose of politics should be to enlarge the spaces in society in which people interact as democratic equals, regardless of inequalities of income and wealth (an argument popularized in 1992 by Kaus in *The End of Equality*). A different but related line of thought emerged in Britain that promoted an 'associational' form of democratic and economic governance (Hirst 1994). Expand the realm of democratic equality, though not necessarily the state, and constrain the extent to which market inequalities pollute the good life, or so went the argument.

In the post-crash era, some of these arguments feel like they belong to a bygone age; and perhaps understandably Hay and Payne do not dwell on any of these antecedents. But there are some commonalities. Each shares a goal with civic capitalism: shaping economic and political structures so they work more directly to enrich the lives of more citizens. Which prompts a prior, and rather prosaic, point: do we even have the societal measures through which to express and gauge that enrichment? After all, it is that which gets measured that counts in political decision-making. To believe otherwise is wishful thinking. The authors recognize the importance of using new approaches to tracking social progress; their sketch of an SED index which would take account of the sustainability and desirability of growth has much to be said for it. But it is crucial to recognize quite how far that sort of approach is from contemporary economic and political decision-making in a mature political economy like that of Britain today.

Currently, we rely on a set of indicators of economic progress which fall woefully short of matching up to today's political rhetoric, never mind a different, more civic-minded one. Despite all the political attention given to issues such as the living standards of those on low or middle incomes, policy is not in any meaningful way guided by any such measure. There is no headline metric of material or social progress for households used to monitor the performance of government. Those that do get used are horribly dated or inadequate. Whereas measures of GDP or the public finances are reported and debated in near-real time, the only reliable information we have on what is happening to middle- or low-income households is always at least several years out of date. Even when we look at something apparently straight-forward, like the level of earnings in the economy, it emerges that in Britain we exclude almost 5 million self-employed workers! It is remarkable that in a data-rich twenty-first-century economy like ours, no one even bothers to attempt to follow what has happened to the earnings of all workers (Kelly 2014a). We cannot therefore begin to move towards a more civic capitalism until we are willing to define, track and then put to use measures of how economic performance is affecting real households and workers across the distribution. That on its own is still some way off.

The arid business of defining the right social and economic goals and measures is, however, only a start. Another plank of a more civic capitalism is an appreciation of how societies and their power structures adjust to new risks that arise from economic change in the form of technology, trade, demographic shifts and so on. Specifically, we might expect that a civic capitalism would examine the scope for, and barriers to, forms of social innovation that help ensure that new economic risks are equitably distributed in society, rather than heavily concentrated on those least able to bear them. Any such inquiry would have to conclude that in Britain there is a lack of social innovation where it is needed.

To make the point, let us return to the example of the rise of the self-employed, one of the more significant, if still under-appreciated, shifts in our jobs market over the last decade. The response in terms of institutions seeking to improve the status, security or collective voice of the self-employed has been striking only by its absence. Existing trades unions have been inert. New civic organizations have failed to emerge. Our political parties have jousted over whether the self-employed should be portrayed as victims of a depression or heroes of an emerging recovery – but none has pursued the task of advocating institutions that would improve their economic well-being.

The same civic innovation gap is also evident in relation to the pressing issue of low pay in Britain. As it happens, the United States is one of the very few OECD countries with a worse track record on low pay than Britain. The structure of its labour market is deeply inhospitable to the plight of the working poor. Yet, despite this, the pressures emerging there through local participatory politics and plebiscites, together with the ascendance of a generation of labour leaders open to innovative methods and resolved to break out of the habit of decades of labour decline, have helped spark a wave of high-energy, high-visibility civic movements that have put low pay on the map (Rolf 2013). This has triggered a ripple of rising minimum wages across major US cities (Kelly 2014b) and spurred the White House to find its voice. By contrast, in Britain, our centralized politics and more con-servative labour movement mean we have not seen an equiv-alent response to a similar social problem. Hay and Payne make a strong case for treating financial innovation with default suspicion; there is an equal need to consider the power imbalances and institutional blockages that are impeding desirable civic innovation.

None of this is to suggest that civic initiative is in any sense a replacement for state action and rule setting. As Hay and Payne note, government regulation that shapes the nature of employment, the control of finance, the governance of companies and the terms of collective bargaining is abso-lutely vital in determining how economic risk and power are distributed in society. But the well-trodden political economy that focuses on these usual suspects is not enough. A civic capitalism should also direct attention to the ease with which social innovation can take place and create the demand and capacity for supportive state action.

Another possibility raised by the 'civic' label is a clear examination of the appropriate boundaries between market, civil society and state. Drawing on the civic liberalism argument, this would point to far greater clarity about the domains in which markets (subject to rules) should be viewed as the dominant form of economic logic and those where they should not.

For example, in the British context, we now have considerable experience of what happens when regulated market capitalism is let rip in the most precarious of sectors. Equally, we also have plenty of form in protecting what might be thought of as capitalistic sectors of the economy from genuine competition and insulating them from risk. It is extraordinary that, for instance, domiciliary care for the elderly is one of the most hyper-atomized, market-driven areas of contemporary economic life with care purchased in real time in micro-slices, and economic risk dumped on vulnerable workers (and therefore on those they care for too). The childcare sector, with its huge churn of 'providers' in and out of the market, is another example. To say that all political parties have been casual about the ethic of care in this country is something of an understatement. Yet if we look elsewhere in our economy, we see that our system of regulation (not to mention direct political influence) has in some sectors – such as retail banking and energy utilities – created a strong bias towards incumbents, with new entrants facing enormous, typically insurmountable, hurdles before they get a chance to compete. It is a familiar refrain in the British context to suggest that we have 'the wrong type of capitalism'; perhaps we also have capitalism in all the wrong places. Civic capitalism should be clear-eyed not just about the need for more regulation but, more particularly, about where in society we want regulation to be market-creating or market-blocking.

Finally, in the next iteration of Hay and Payne's thinking, we would encourage them to explore what their reform programme means for politics: civic capitalism surely demands a more civic state. Setting out a programme of reforms for capitalism is one thing. Combining it with a clear line of sight to the nature of the political leadership, policy-making culture, societal coalitions and sources of public legitimacy that might conceivably sustain these reforms is quite another.

The risk here is that civic capitalism ends up as an attractive reform programme dependent on a statist model of policy and a largely discredited view of how lasting political change is secured. It is interesting to note the mini-trend towards former policy-makers – typically those who were involved in shaping large, progressive policy reforms, some of which only existed for several years before then being dismantled – now beginning to reflect hard on the lessons of their governing experience (Mulgan 2010; Pearce 2014; Taylor 2014). The thread running through these interesting contributions is a sharp sense of the limitations, contradictions and lack of political rootedness of many centrally led reform programmes. Whether or not one signs up to the entirety of these critiques, they serve as a useful reminder of the problems of making an argument about reforming capitalism without simultaneously engaging with the nature of the political leadership and culture needed to sustain and legitimize the proposed programme.

In sum, civic capitalism needs a parallel argument about a civic state. Hay and Payne's noble agenda will not be carved out of the dead wood of our existing politics. Let us hope this is the theme of their next contribution.

Why Not Frighten the Horses?

Ruth Levitas

The essence of civic capitalism is 'the governance of the market, by the state, in the name of the people, to deliver collective public goods, equity and social justice'. Hay and Payne rightly argue that 'the market is never and can never be a guarantor of equity or justice', deducing that 'social and economic justice' must be 'imposed upon the market by the state in our name'. It would be a fine thing indeed if the principles of civic capitalism were to underpin the Labour Party's manifesto for the 2015 election. For what could we then expect? A commitment to much more effective regulation of market activity, both within states and internationally; a commitment to environmentally sustainable growth; a commitment to new measures of growth and development, which include environmental and social factors as well as the purely economic; and a commitment to a radical reduction in inequality, both within and between states. This would return the Labour Party's programme almost to the recommendations of John Smith's Commission on Social Justice, set up in 1992 but reporting after the 'New Labour' takeover in 1994 (see Levitas 2005 [1998]). The mantra of economic efficiency and social justice never, of course, properly interrogated the potential conflict between these or the direction in which that conflict was systematically resolved. Civic capitalism would not, however, return the Labour Party to the demands of Clause IV, section 4, which, prior to Blair's hijacking, appeared on every member's card: 'To secure for the workers by hand or by brain the full fruits of their industry and the most equitable distribution thereof that may be possible upon the basis of the common owner-ship of the means of production, distribution, and exchange, and the best obtainable system of popular administration thereof.' And that is because Hay and Payne nowhere discuss questions of ownership, which are fundamental to the nature of capitalism itself, a point to which I will return. Their attempt to reclaim social democracy, albeit limited, is surely to be welcomed. In particular, I agree with Hay and Payne's emphasis on the positive role of the state, the necessity for regulation, the importance of environmental limits, the need for different measures of growth and sustainability and the pressing need to reduce levels of inequality. But, for reasons of space, I am going to focus on my reservations about Hay and Payne's general approach.

First, the model of social change embedded here is wholly idealist: everything is a matter of values, of ideology, rather than material practices and social relations. We have to replace one ideology of capitalism with a new and different one, and one set of 'principles' with another. Thus they con-strue the problem of the last couple of decades as one in which 'we' were all taken in by the merits of markets and, although regretting rising inequality, believed it a necessary price to pay for economic growth.

Speak for yourself: I was never part of this 'we'. Nor did all 'mainstream commentators' buy into this view. There have been persistent (and institutionally specific) arguments in favour of regulation, for example by Will Hutton. Roy Hattersley never shifted his position in relation to the impor-tance of equality. Polly Toynbee wrote consistently about both regulation and inequality throughout the Blair years. Among social policy experts, the most prominent advocates of greater equality were people like Peter Townsend and

Ruth Lister. Richard Wilkinson and Kate Pickett's (2009) book, *The Spirit Level*, brought into public view work that Wilkinson had been doing for twenty-five years. One of the most trenchant critics of the neoliberal takeover at the global level has been Naomi Klein (2007). Recent dissidents include Stewart Lansley (2006, 2012), Robert Peston (2008), Thomas Piketty (2014) and Owen Jones (2014). And the case of Hutton is instructive in another way: mainstream commentators who might have hoped for influence after the 1997 'Labour' victory, but did not buy in to the neoliberal myth, were relatively marginalized. This reflects processes of power in the print and broadcast media, again related to questions of ownership, and also the increasing class closure of the professions, especially journalism.

Second, some might object to Hay and Payne's approach on the grounds that it is 'utopian', as indeed it is. It articulates a better model of society, not just as a method of illuminating the ills of the present, but as a putative goal. In principle, I am in favour of a carefully considered utopian approach, as I have argued strongly in my 2013 *Utopia as Method* (Levitas 2013). But such an approach is intrinsically sociological, and needs to be formulated at the level of social practices and social institutions. Indeed, as Roberto Unger argues, this process needs to be a collective one arising out of democratic experimentalism and collective improvisation, which themselves open up both new perspectives and new real possibilities (Unger 1998, 2007). Hay and Payne's approach has all the weaknesses of utopian political theory in remaining at the level of principles, rather than institutions and practices. There is a very short reference to the 'social' as some kind of add-on to be elaborated by experts in social policy (no mention of sociologists!). Remaining at this abstract level allows Hay and Payne to make the mistake of supposing economic, political and social processes to be different, and to forget that economic policy is also social policy. This is evident both in the consequences of austerity for the poorest in Britain and the less visible class re-composition among the very rich, resulting

from untrammelled inequality and regressive taxation policies. The pincer movement of these trends in relation to
house prices and economic stability also illustrates that the
economic is social, and vice versa.

Third, Hay and Payne seem to buy into the self-serving
fiction of neoliberalism that it rolled back the influence of
the state. As analyses of Thatcherism in the 1980s were clear,
the free economy was necessarily supported by state appa-
ratuses. The state was, and continues to be, involved in
legislation restricting trade union activity, public assembly
and protest, and freedom of movement. The restriction of
civil liberties by the state, sometimes under the guise of anti-
terrorism, has been ongoing since 1979. The state is currently implicated in the enforcement of welfare cuts and thus
the rise in destitution and food banks, in the intrusive and
scurrilous 'troubled families' agenda, and in the failure to
collect taxes from Amazon, Starbucks and the like. So the
question is not whether we prefer neoliberalism and a small,
non-interventionist state or social democracy with a larger,
interventionist one, but how (or if) we can make the state a
force for the common good in a capitalist economy.

Fourth, the weaknesses of abstraction afflict also the discussion of measures of economic growth. Hay and Payne
rightly argue that different measures that incorporate environmental impacts and social development are necessary.
Measures such as the Index of Social and Economic Welfare
(ISEW) and the Measure of Domestic Progress (MDP) have
existed long prior to Stiglitz and Sen's attempts to integrate
them into international development measures; they are pio-
neered in Britain by the New Economics Foundation. Their
limitation is that they can distract attention from the very
material inequalities civic capitalism needs to reduce. But
Hay and Payne's account is rooted too much in the question
of measures and insufficiently in the actual processes that
are being measured. Consequently, it omits some of the
major problems with GDP as a measure of growth. One of
these is its absurd inclusion of all market activity, however
harmful: British GDP has just been revised upwards by the

inclusion of the estimated values of drug dealing and pros-
titution and has always included legitimate harms such as
alcohol and tobacco production together with the costs of
their ill effects. The corresponding exclusion of all non-
market work creates its own absurdities, exposing fundamental gender inequities both in actual social processes and
in the way in which they are measured (Levitas 2013; Waring
1989). The questions of growth, development, what we mean
by these, and their relationship to building equitable and
sustainable societies are absolutely vital. But the emphasis
needs to be on the institutional framework itself.

Fifth, Hay and Payne miss completely one of the central
reasons why 'growth' is so important to conventional economics and politics. To be sure, it is partly because professional economists deal in snake oil and mirrors, and
politicians are often prisoners of ill-considered orthodoxies.
But growth has a very important ideological function, and
that is to disguise the process of rising inequality and the
concentration of capital. If there is growth, living standards
can rise while wealth continues to become more concentrated. If growth stalls, the illusion that everyone benefits
can be sustained for a time on the basis of easy credit and
rising consumer debt, while profits continue to accumulate.
But lack of growth and increasing debt eventually expose the
extent of inequality and its increase. It is this, and not a
moral transformation, that has brought the issue of inequality tentatively back on to the political agenda.

Lastly, and most importantly, there is the question of the
viability of civic capitalism as a vision and basis of an alternative world order. Hay and Payne's intentions in describing
their model as 'civic capitalism' are not completely clear; and
they are unclear precisely because the model remains abstract
and therefore unspecific about actual institutional arrangements, especially concerning ownership and power. But is
this a genuine alternative, branded as a variety of capitalism
in order not to frighten the horses? If so, the paradox is that,
while claiming radical difference, the nomenclature of civic
capitalism discursively reprises the view that there is indeed

no alternative to capitalism, so we should pursue a kinder, regulated version. And it assumes that there is a common interest in such a stabilized system.

Sociologically, the model here corresponds to a quite old-fashioned functionalism, in which potential conflicts of interests are balanced and regulated by a benign state working for the common good. And yet there are many reasons to suppose that this is not how capitalist societies, whether at the national or the global level, actually work. Strong contemporary arguments come from writers like Thomas Piketty whose importance lies in his demonstration not just of the extent of inequality but of the intrinsic trend of capitalism towards its increase. David Harvey (2010) argues similarly that capitalism depends on constant expansion of markets and on 3 per cent compound growth, rendering capitalism and sustainability fundamentally incompatible. While, of course, as discussed above, it depends what you mean by growth, the basic drivers of capitalism are expansion and capital accumulation. Globalization is better understood as imperialism, the highest stage of capitalism: more and more capital is located in fewer and fewer hands, whilst multinational corporations control more and more of the world's resources. Is regulation, through states and international institutions, a sufficient answer to the problem of repossessing the world's wealth for the benefit of ordinary people? Who will expropriate the expropriators? And Wolfgang Streeck (2014a, 2014b) argues that since the 1970s we have been witnessing the declining capacity of states to manage the growing fundamental conflict between a capitalist economy and democratic polity. This has been brought to a head by the present threefold crisis of low growth and capital accumulation, burgeoning inequality and intensified distributional conflicts, and the persistent rise in overall indebtedness. For Streeck, capitalism is most likely to prevail, although it is simultaneously at risk of collapse, and 'even capitalism's master technicians have no clue today how to make the system whole again' (Streeck 2014a: 46). Streeck says we have to learn to contemplate the end of capitalism without being able to answer the question of what to put in its place, and without the comforting fiction that such a collapse will only happen when a collective subject is ready to redeem our common fate.

As a proponent of utopianism, both as imagination and as praxis, I, like Hay and Payne, think we must go on trying to set out alternatives and consider the potential agents of change. But I also think these must actually be alternatives to capitalism, not modified versions of it, and must be presented as such. In this process, we have to address questions of wealth and power and the nature of existing and potential social institutions. And 'we' needs continuing interrogation. Even Occupy's contrast between the 1 per cent and the 99 per cent does not adequately address the conflicts of interests that will have to be overcome, the solidarities that will need to be built or the risks of failure that lie ahead.

It's the Democratic Politics, Stupid!

Mick Moran

One of the most striking, and depressing, developments in the social sciences in recent decades has been the way professional social scientists have turned away from large issues of social organization and social justice. The impulses that gave rise to the social sciences in universities in the first half of the twentieth century were closely connected to wider social conditions and were reformist and radical in character. The professionalization of disciplines and the growth in scale of academic empires narrowed the concerns of social scientists, perhaps nowhere more so than in the field of economics, which largely severed its historical connections with the socially informed discipline of political economy. Hay and Payne's essay is thus a triply welcoming sign: it comes out of an institute which seeks to revive the classical concerns of political economy; it addresses issues of great social concern in an accessible and committed language; and, perhaps most important of all, it thinks big, making arguments for fundamental reconstruction of economic practices on a global scale. Anything further from the cautious narrowness of most contemporary social science would be hard to imagine. It is not necessary to agree with all, or indeed most, of what they say to realize that this is an entirely healthy development, and that their essay amounts to a serious and substantial intervention in public debate.

Like all ambitious projects, Hay and Payne's paper also has problems. The big problem lies not in its vision of the different future. Every reader will dissent in some particular way from what they prescribe. (This one does not share fully their enthusiasm for the world of the green people.) But most readers, most of the time, will be convinced by their alternative vision and will applaud their intellectual adventurousness in taking risks to develop it. The big problem, as they plainly realize themselves, is turning vision into reality: into getting from A to Z, so to speak. Hay and Payne seem to have two solutions to this problem, one explicit and one implicit. The explicit solution is in part defensive. This paper, they say, offers a 'model of capitalism': it 'will not and cannot tell us exactly what policies to follow in detail in every ... situation ... the task of setting out a new model of capitalism is more like designing a new car than offering advice to the driver from the passenger seat – and arguably there has been rather a lot of that already.' Let us not press this analogy too far, but the drift of their argument is clear. What is on offer in the paper is 'a plausible narrative that explains to the citizens of our model capitalism what they are part of, how they might fit in, what gives their productive lives some meaning. ... Capitalism needs to be seen to have a moral purpose and we need to be as clear about that moral purpose as we can be.' The explicit answer therefore seems to involve narrowing the mandate of the paper: they are designing the car, not saying anything about the identity of the driver or the short-term direction of travel. But implicitly this also relies on a famous model of the connection between intellectual argument and political outcomes, one voiced most elegantly by Keynes: the social scientist as academic scribbler. This is how he put it: 'The ideas of economists and political philosophers, both when they are right and when they are wrong, are more powerful than is commonly understood ... Madmen in authority, who hear voices in the air, are distilling their frenzy from some academic scribbler of a few years back' (Keynes 1936: 383).

The Surprising Neglect of Politics

Thus Hay and Payne have two solutions to the problem of how their vision might be translated into reality, and they are linked: as academic scribblers they are offering a moral vision of the future of the capitalist economy without attempting to prescribe the specifics of how that economy might in day-to-day fashion be steered. This is a surprising position when we know the identities of these authors because they are, of course, two distinguished political scientists (or, if that seems overly professionalized, two distinguished observers of our politics, in Britain, Europe and globally). Yet the conception of civic capitalism offered in the paper – the key to the alternative vision of how we might recon-struct a capitalist order – actually has very little to say about politics: which is to say, without pressing their original analogy too far, that it has oddly little to say about the identity of the driver(s) of the capitalist vehicle or about how they might be chosen. That neglect is immediately clear in the very way they identify the 'civic' in capitalism. Given the etymology of the word, and the connotations of everyday usage, one might expect 'civic capitalism' to have something very explicit to say about how civic authority is to be organ-ized. It does not. Instead, it offers an account of the relation-ship between the state and the economy, as follows: 'the very nature of civic capitalism [involves] – the governance of the market, by the state, in the name of the people, to deliver collective public goods, equity and social justice.' Now what is striking about this is that it implies plenty about the moral purpose of government, but says nothing about how govern-ment is to be organized to achieve that moral purpose. That bias is evident throughout the rest of the paper. Bar some fairly modest proposals late in the paper for the reform of institutions of global economic government, there is virtually nothing about the reform of political institutions – though a great deal recommending the expansion of the responsibilities of the state, notably via more regulation, and a reorientation of its substantive purpose (for instance in the creation of a more environmentally sustainable economy). Hay and Payne have thus offered a compelling vision of what a capitalism infused with civic purpose might look like: compelling in the sense that the reader is compelled by the argument, or compelled to resist their vision by offering some alternative. But, in the oddest of omissions, they have almost nothing to say about how civic authority might be reconstructed in this system of civic capitalism.

Hay and Payne might respond to this criticism by simply saying, 'Give us a break. We have already offered a wholesale redesign of the moral purpose of a market economy in one fairly short paper. We cannot be expected to reconstruct political institutions as well.' Their difficulty, though, is that, without this political reconstruction, their economic reconstruction has little hope of being realized. They will suffer the fate of Keynes's academic scribblers. They will have influence, but their work will be the 'voices in the air' distilled by madmen (and women) in authority. And the distillation will almost certainly not be a distillation of the essence of what Hay and Payne want to argue.

To work out what needs to be done to reconstruct civic authority under capitalism, Hay and Payne will not need to look far. They can just glance at their own bookshelves to see what Hay has written about the decay of public authority in modern democracies, and what Payne has written about the pathologies of the politics of development (e.g. Hay 2007; Payne 2005). In the few words available to me, I cannot do more than sketch what is needed in the areas with which I am most familiar, the liberal democracies anatomized so insightfully by Hay. What our understanding of modern capitalist democracy surely makes clear is that the economic and social pathologies which Hay and Payne seek to remedy have not dropped from heaven; they are the product of, and are reinforced by, pathological political configurations. This suggests to me that Hay and Payne need above all to go on to sketch out at least a vision of how civic authority could be reconstructed. If they do not, they will assuredly remain in the realm of academic scribbling as described by Keynes.

What's Wrong with Civic Authority?

Here are three areas where the findings of modern political science suggest that the civic realm needs reconstructing if Hay and Payne's economic and social vision is to stand some hope of realization.

First, the reconstruction of party institutions. The mass party with roots in civil society, and drawing its main resources from civil society, was a key institution in the realization of a democratically functioning civic realm. We know very well what has become of it. The parties that claim authority to implement, or not, the kinds of policies that Hay and Payne advocate are shrivelled and eviscerated: shrivelled because, almost uniformly across the advanced capitalist world, they no longer have any real healthy roots in civil society as their membership has shrunk to a geriatric core of activists and an elite cadre of professional politicians; eviscerated as their internal life has come to be dominated either by corporate funders or by the funding state. These are the 'drivers' that Hay and Payne are content to let control the new machine of civic capitalism which they are so carefully designing.

Second, the reconstruction of the institutions of popular participation beyond parties. We again know very well what has happened, and the pattern is almost universal across advanced capitalist democracies. The classic institution of civic decision – the competitive election – exercises a decreasing hold over populations, and in part as a result has descended into a contest between elites employing the manipulative soft technologies of electioneering: policies designed to track opinion polls and the responses of focus groups; the segmenting of the civic sphere into subsets of groups targeted using the technologies of marketing; and the transformation of political debate into manipulated media opportunities and contrived encounters between political elites and normal citizens. Alongside this has grown popular cynicism about the public sphere ('why we hate politics'), coupled with a kind of Wild West world populated by single-issue politics and an increasingly vicious subculture of political argument in social media.

Third, the reconstruction of institutions of civic decision-making. The country in which Hay and Payne's paper is published is a paradigm of what has gone wrong. There is little point in endowing governing institutions with enhanced regulatory authority and added moral purpose if those institutions are controlled by a metropolitan elite with an established history of perpetrating policy fiascos (see, for instance, King and Crewe 2013). What has happened to local government in Britain is emblematic of the problem: traditions of civic creativity and activism have been stifled from a centre intent on exercising control, often in the interests of winning those electoral contests fought under the conditions I have just described. (I use 'Britain' advisedly because the creation of devolved institutions in Scotland has been accompanied by a centralization of power, but this time on Edinburgh rather than London.) The result is well known. Just as popular participation is marked by a separation between the official world of democratic politics and the Wild West world of unofficial participation, so across Europe the wielders of centralized authority are losing control to sub-national territorial separatism.

It's the Democratic Politics, Stupid!

It was, famously though perhaps apocryphally, in the campaign headquarters of candidate Bill Clinton – a consummate practitioner of the debased manipulative politics of modern democracy – in the 1992 US presidential election that there hung the injunction to remember 'It's the economy, stupid!' But, for Hay and Payne, the slogan now has to be:

'it's the democratic politics, stupid!' They do indeed now have a blueprint for reforming the economy and culture of capitalism. Like all blueprints, it will need refining, and not everyone will want to sign up to all the details. That does not matter. But what does matter is that they have little chance of turning their blueprint into some sort of working mechanism if they do not attend at the same time to what should be the core of civic capitalism: how it organizes the most important part of the civic realm, the political domain.

Recasting Neoliberal Mindsets

Ann Pettifor

Hay and Payne must be congratulated for their initiative: to develop an alternative, progressive narrative that will substitute for the mawkish 'analysis of the failings of the [now infamous] Anglo-liberal model of capitalism'.

A *coherent* alternative and progressive economic narrative is something that the Labour movement, the Green movement and many other progressive movements yearn for. For this narrative to be coherent, it obviously has to be based on sound analysis. But it has also to *reframe* the key concepts underpinning neoliberal ideology, and the language used to reinforce the dominance of neoliberalism.

As Professor George Lakoff argues in his book, *Don't Think of an Elephant!* (2004):

> Frames facilitate our most basic interactions with the world – they structure our ideas and concepts, they shape the way we reason, and they even impact how we perceive and how we act ...
>
> For the most part, our use of frames is unconscious and automatic – we use them without realizing it.

Key examples of words that reinforce existing conventional analysis and framing of economic issues, and that are included in Hay and Payne's narrative, are 'regulation', 'growth' and 'global'. I will argue in this brief comment that, for an alternative economic narrative to be coherent and effective, we need to abandon the framing implied by this language, and replace these words not just with alternative language but also with an alternative analysis.

'Regulation'

This is a word that progressives favour – one that neoliberal economists have succeeded in capturing and negating. Hay and Payne argue (wrongly in my view) that: 'the truth is that there was always something in the argument that regulation has a certain propensity to suppress growth – or, at least, some forms of growth. And growth is, of course, what incumbent administrations … crave above all else.' They then go on to sound defensive, suggesting that we need 'to adopt a principle of discretionary precaution in economic regulation'. This defensive approach *makes* and reinforces the argument made by orthodox economists and their friends in the finance sector: that regulation suppresses 'growth' or economic activity.

The term 'regulation' implies a micro-economic approach to the management of the international financial and trading system. Such micro-management can always be distorted and manipulated. Above all, it can serve to divide and rule both national and international regulators. Republican Jeb Hensarling ('first elected to Congress in 2002, a strong conservative and an outspoken advocate for limited government and unlimited opportunity': Hensarling 2014), and now chairman of the US Congress's Financial Services Committee, trashes the Dodd–Frank Wall Street Reform Act with these words: 'The Dodd–Frank Act, signed into law in July 2010, spans 2,300 pages and directs federal regulators to burden job creators and the economy with more than 400 new rules and mandates.'

No finessing of language here; but Hensarling is not alone. Dodd–Frank is frequently used as an example of excessive regulation and bureaucracy, when it is clearly an example of regulation deliberately throttled at birth and made unworkable by its Wall Street opponents.

But to be hung up on regulation is to be trapped in the flawed micro-economic worldview of orthodox economics. To micro-manage global, footloose finance is to be trapped in the web of financial complexity created by *haute finance*. The international and supranational financial system does not only need to be micro-managed; above all, it needs macro-management.

So I suggest that progressives should instead be writing and talking about planning and building a new *international monetary architecture* within which the financial system will be required to operate. Once a proper and sound international monetary system and architecture is designed, with clear rules for its *management* (not regulation), then how it is regulated at a local level can be left to the wisdom of democratically elected local politicians and the public authorities they will lead. It is the overall monetary architecture that will in effect bring about the transformation of an unruly, ungoverned financial system.

Ed Conway's recent book – *The Summit* (2014) – on the Bretton Woods Conference of 1944 reminds us that the international architecture designed at that event did not involve micro-regulation. Private bankers were denied the opportunities provided by US Congressional debates around Dodd–Frank – they were simply excluded from the Bretton Woods Conference by the president of the United States! The vision of an international monetary system or architecture that the public authorities would manage, and within which the private finance sector would be required to operate, is a vision, an international architecture to which we should once again aspire. After all, it led to what most economists define as the 'golden age' of economics.

In order to maintain today's conditions of unfettered international capital mobility, orthodox economists prefer to confine and narrow debate to the domestic regulation of the finance sector. By doing so, they draw us all into a neurological, linguistic and analytical framing trap.

'Growth'

Growth – defined as the long-term expansion of a country's productive potential – is a word rightly abhorred by environmentalists. It is a word based on the flawed logic that, unlike the finite natural world, the economy can only continue to expand, endlessly. Unlike all that is natural, 'economic growth' does not appear to be subject to the laws of thermodynamics, according to prominent environmental economists like Herman Daly.

The term 'growth' – now so potent in economic discourse – entered the picture only relatively recently. In an earlier age, and after the cataclysm of the Depression, full employment was the most important economic goal. Economists assessed, measured and sought to manage the *level* of economic activity required to achieve full employment.

In the 1960s, the emphasis changed. 'Growth' entered the picture and full employment fell away as a policy goal. Today 'growth' and inequality have become major preoccupations. An alternative progressive narrative could once again place full employment at the centre of economic debate and seek to ensure that policy is oriented not towards 'growth' alone but rather towards maintaining *levels* of economic activity that ensure full employment, financial stability and environmental sustainability.

'Global'

'Global' and 'globalization' are words much used by those economists and policy-makers concerned to protect, I would argue, the *supranational* status of multinational corporations, in particular financial institutions. A global company should be free to operate, it is assumed, above and beyond the democratic oversight of nations in which it is free to trade and profit. And, if such freedom enables 'global' companies to evade or avoid taxation in those states in which it is not headquartered, then so be it.

A progressive narrative would not fall into the intellectual trap of accepting the notion that a company, or any other being, can be 'global' – beyond the oversight of states. Instead, companies should once again be defined as 'international' organizations – with the emphasis on the coordination and cooperation implied in the word 'international'.

As again Lakoff argues: 'Reframing *is* social change.' If the 'now infamous Anglo-liberal model of capitalism' is to be transformed, progressive thinkers must change the way we think about, and give expression to, an alternative.

What Has to Be Civilized?

Matthew Watson

Any attempt to go beyond saying what is wrong in current circumstances to speculating how things might be different is always to be welcomed. Crisis Britain, after all, has become a front for the turn towards an increasingly Nasty Britain. In this context, Colin Hay and Anthony Payne's desire to seize the political agenda in the cause of civic capitalism is particularly noteworthy. It is admirable in its own terms because it sets out an alternative vision of how we might allow ourselves to live that stands directly at odds with the political and cultural trends of the last forty years. But it is doubly admirable in taking a direct shot at those who would preach collective sacrifice as crisis response whilst carefully singling out the unorganized and voiceless to carry a disproportionate burden of contemporary economic restructuring.

The broad political objectives that lie in the background of the Hay and Payne paper have my full support. However, it is the responsibility of fellow travellers to question one another's strategy of problem specification in the interests of introducing greater analytical clarity into the debate. It is in this spirit that my comments are presented.

My main concern is with what happens to Hay and Payne's carefully thought-through reform agenda if the object of that reform is not as they specify it. The reader learns much about what it would take to promote a distinctly civic variant of capitalism, and the resulting vision is certainly one in which an increasingly civilized tone will be struck in the relationship between one person and another, as well as between people and nature. An instinct to care is being promoted, one where voluntary acquiescence to the new norm would be the first-best option but where behavioural change through legal statute is a more than acceptable second best. However, halting the advance of market ideology cannot be relied upon, on its own, to civilize everyday economic relations. But I do worry that the economic structures of contemporary British capitalism do not look like those of the classical market stereotype and that this might make access to the civic mission very difficult indeed. Let me now try to explain the basis of my concerns, whilst at the same time – as all fellow travellers should be prepared to do – making suggestions for the way forward.

At-a-Distance Accumulation and the Civic Mission

It took me a little by surprise that there were only two clearly apparent time-specific qualifiers to an undifferentiated notion of capitalism in the Hay and Payne paper. One refers to the predominantly neoliberal strategy of political governance in evidence since the 1970s and the other to the pathologies of what they call the 'Anglo-liberal growth model'. However, the former tends to capture only the political priorities of the regulatory form within which the economic essence evolves, and not the resulting outcomes. The latter, in turn, emphasizes the limits of successfully incorporating a winning political coalition into an increasingly financialized economy. Both are clearly worthy of greater public attention, but neither really gets to the heart of how the structures of the British economy have changed in recent decades.

The type of qualifier that to me seems to be most in need of addition would speak directly to the balance of ownership within the economy. The demise of what might be called 'high-street capitalism' is reflected in the related rise of two new consumption spaces. One emerges from the replacement of independently owned stores with national or even international chains that look and feel exactly the same wherever they are experienced. The accent of the shop assistant might change, but what they sell on behalf of faraway shareholders and how they are allowed to sell it remain resolutely the same. The other new consumption space is – it hardly needs saying – the internet, and it has taken retail homogeneity to whole new levels. Even the local accent disappears, as all that matters is the voice in your own head telling you whether this is indeed the bargain being proclaimed.

What unites these seemingly disparate trends is that they place the mundane activities of everyday economic life increasingly at a distance from those who own the means of production. It is clear from the Hay and Payne paper that their civic mission takes the level of mundane economic activities extremely seriously. There is a tension here, though, in that so many of the practices of everyday economic life have been devolved to the individual, cocooning them seemingly in a world of their own, but that this has brought them no closer to where power is exercised at the level of economic structure. They might well be choosing between alternatives on an informed basis, much in the mould of the classical market-bound agent acting in a context of many buyers and many sellers, but the limits of their choices are apparent.

There are some product lines that do allow people to express themselves as ethical and environmentally conscious consumers, and in these purchases it is possible to see the outline of civic capitalism come into view. But such products represent the exception of niche consumption, rather than being the rule. In the general case, choice tends to be restricted to selecting between different price cues in the context of relatively homogeneous products mass produced by companies that refuse to act as though they are part of the local community. It is only the exceptional type of consumption that provides the individual with a sense that they are interacting economically with other people and that their decisions therefore have distinctly human consequences. The general type of consumption, by contrast, seems to be governed by abstract conceptions of price and draws individuals into the clutches of a corporate world in which their lived economic experiences become increasingly detached from the feeling that those experiences involve other people. In other words, it is only the exceptional type of consumption that is typically performed in a behavioural space in which civic norms are unambiguously present. Following the demise of 'high-street capitalism', the general type of consumption is typically performed in an altogether different behavioural space, where even the possibility of civic capitalism might be too remote for comfort.

The changing structure of ownership therefore clearly matters to the possibilities for civic capitalism. This is not to collapse the debate into a politically sterile nostalgia for pristine, small-scale, localized circuits of production and consumption which perhaps never existed anyway in that form. The accumulation imperative has been ever-present in all economic forms that prioritize private over collective ownership. The objective has always been to make money, which is as true of a future civic capitalism as it is of today's corporate bypassing of the classical market stereotype. The only questions are: (1) how that money is made in the interests of meeting the accumulation imperative; and (2) whether this is detrimental to forging a concrete civic rationality out of the increasingly abstract economic rationalities that shape the contours of mundane economic experiences in Britain today. This, to my mind in any case, is why more emphasis in the debate needs to be placed on the structure of ownership. The production of price-sensitive but socially abstracted consumers has played a large part in the legitimation of the corporate bypassing of the classical market stereotype: so much so that the two now seem to be co-constitutive of one another. What scope is there for moving on from this situation, which seems so ill-suited to the embedding of civic norms?

Market Escapees as Obstacles to Civic-Oriented Regulation

There are numerous very important observations in the Hay and Payne paper about the need not to simply take markets for granted. All of these points are well made, and once again the only difference I have with them on this issue is a matter of emphasis. How might we begin to think about the limits of markets, and what might be done to create a potentially popular reform programme through specifying clearly where those limits are presumed to lie? Hay and Payne tend to reduce these questions to the need for a more assertively interventionist structure of governance, one which revolves around demonstrating that the state can be held to account for enhancing well-being much more effectively under civic capitalism than under whatever we can call the system we have today. I worry, though, that the degree of change they envision requires something much more profound than that. Arming the state with new capabilities and asking citizens to judge it on its performance must be bolstered very much by getting people to reflect really quite systematically on what it means to be a citizen within a modern economic setting. Yet here we come across a potential paradox that it will be necessary to unravel if civic capitalism is to take root.

Some extremely significant academic work has been undertaken recently on the generalized acceptance that a collectively experienced fiscal consolidation is necessary if the economy is to be given the breathing space to rise again from the ashes of the financial crisis (Konings 2012; Stanley 2014). Opinion poll data confirm that this is a developing trend, with more and more people reporting that they believe austerity is a necessary evil in the national interest of repairing broken markets (YouGov 2010). This would appear to be evidence of something approaching mass ideological buy-in to the idea that 'the market' is now the public good that trumps all others in providing rights of economic citizenship. Might it even be possible to go as far as to posit the presence of a 'market citizenry' for whom state interventions

in the name of civic capitalism might represent incursions
into what they expect to receive as citizens? Whatever the
answer to this question, the broader point surely remains
valid. Irrespective of the effect that the ensuing situation has
had on their personal life chances, there is a widely held
feeling – cautious in its articulation but producing real effects
nonetheless – that 'the market' somehow represents the fur-
thest reaches of human economic aspiration. The cultural
politics of Thatcherism thus remain deeply institutionalized
at the individual level and pose an obvious problem for any
mode of citizenship built consciously upon limiting the scope
of markets.

The paradox here is that it is something very different to
'the market' that the vast majority of people experience in
Britain today when going about their everyday economic
affairs. The language of the market remains paramount, as
increasingly does the image of economic citizenship it is used
to promote. But still this is all very different to saying that
people *experience* market institutions in their daily life to
the same extent that their lives are *thought about* using
market frames of reference. Despite the prevalence of market
ideology since the 1970s, the economic structure that has
evolved in its wake might more usefully be conceptualized
in terms of its distinctly non-market institutions. The architects of civic capitalism will be confronted with a context in
which power is exercised to escape genuinely market-based
relationships. It is only those who lack such power that have
to deal with the day-to-day realities of market imperatives.
The powerful receive a distinctly anti-civic helping hand to
circumvent market imperatives, and it is these actors and not
the market per se that need to be subject to new forms of
regulation in the first instance.

This is by no means a call for more regulation *by* the
market, but it does show that regulation *of* the market is not
necessarily a self-evident panacea. The key in this regard
seems to be the degree of incorporation into the market prior
to the new regulation. If it is something less than all-
encompassing, then state interventions simply to limit the

size, scope and reach of markets might not have the desired effect. Indeed, they could even miss their target altogether. Civic capitalism might very well work best when governing face-to-face economic relations in which it is immediately obvious how the civic mission can be expected to benefit all involved. But it is precisely this sort of face-to-face relationship that is ruled out when economic power is exercised at a distance by market escapees. Market escapees might end up being more of an impediment to the successful introduction of civic capitalism than the market institutions against which the possibilities of civic capitalism are currently being thought through.

Conclusion

I am a relatively easy convert to the abstract idea of civic capitalism, especially in circumstances in which the choice boils down to that or more of the same. Even if its ambitions are limited to an incrementalism that will leave radically transformative change long in the making, it still deserves support as an antidote to what we have today. The Hay and Payne paper can serve as an important rallying point for harnessing disappointment, frustration and even resentment at how much of everyday economic life is now conducted in an anonymized and depersonalized manner. There is a potential world out there to discover which exists beyond the touch of a computer screen, the bland homogenization of mass consumption culture and the gratuitous spectacles of financial excess. The authors invite us to begin exploring new political spaces within which such a world might be activated. Most importantly, their paper holds open the possibility of dignifying anew everyday economic relations and recognizing the efforts that people make to negotiate even the most mundane aspects of livelihood struggles.

If any of what I have said in the preceding pages is in any way correct, though, there are as yet unresolved tensions that first have to be tackled. Perhaps most significantly, if civic capitalism is to open up unambiguously progressive political spaces, something must be done about those who have positioned themselves in the name of commercial self-interest beyond market logic and, in many cases, also seemingly above the law. It is surely ironic that this almost certainly means first bringing those ostensibly all-powerful actors back into the market fold before market logic can be subjected to a much-needed dose of the civic mission. Leaving them to continue roaming freely as market escapees will facilitate the circumvention of the normalizing pressures of civic capitalism just as effectively as happens under whatever we choose to call today's system of capitalism in Britain.

Part III

Building Civic Capitalism

Towards Civic
Capitalism in Britain

Colin Hay and Anthony Payne

Our aim in this little book has been to make the case for an alternative to the excesses of the Anglo-liberal model of capitalism whose pathologies and globally contagious effects the crisis exposed so glaringly. We have done so as clearly as we can and in relatively general terms. As such, although focused on Britain and frequently illustrated with respect to the British case, our argument is, we hope, readily generalizable beyond the Anglo-liberal core of a globalization process still (alas) largely conducted in Anglo-liberal terms.

But in this final part our task is a little different. In it we seek to address ourselves more directly to the distinctiveness and immediateness of Britain's particular plight today and to the crucial question of what can and must be done quickly to begin to rectify this. 'Here' and 'now' may well not be a very good place to start in making the transition to a civic capitalism, but it is precisely where we must start since it is the only place we *can* start. Indeed, the difficulty of getting from here and now to 'there' – and the sense that the distance that needs to be travelled is growing with every passing day – makes it all the more imperative to focus on what can and must be done immediately. That is the task that we set ourselves in this final chapter. We start by setting out the situation, as we see it, in which we find ourselves today, with Britain on the eve of the 2015 general election.

Any way one looks at it (and whether gauged in conventional terms or in terms of the alternative currency of global economic success we have proposed), the long-term prospects of the British economy look pretty bleak in the absence of some quite seismic shifts in economic thinking and economic policy practice. Yes, it might be protested, growth has returned, inflation is low, unemployment is falling and there is no immediate prospect of a steep upward trajectory in interest rates. But, as even the governor of the Bank of England (Mark Carney) and the chancellor of the exchequer (George Osborne) in their different ways have both now conceded (see Carney 2014; Osborne 2014), the growth we have looks alarmingly unstable and would appear to be predicated on the inflation of an all-too-familiar asset-price bubble centred on the housing market. That is why the coalition government's much-touted 'Help to Buy' scheme, though not yet abandoned, has been in the dock and why the chancellor's 2014 Mansion House speech freely conceded the need of the Bank of England to cap mortgage loan-to-value ratios to temper the overheating in the housing market. Of course, it encouraged the governor to do so not quite yet ... and, indeed, not in any way capable of yielding tangible effects (and thereby suppressing growth) before the general election.

This is alarming for two reasons. First, and perhaps most obviously, it suggests (in what is perhaps now a familiar theme of our argument) that Britain's seemingly good economic performance since 2013 is in fact a chimera – and that the quite conscious pump-priming of the housing market has merely served to mask the persistence of long-standing structural pathologies that remain almost entirely unaddressed. The growth crisis, in effect, has not been resolved – and that makes the debt crisis much, much more difficult to deal with in the medium term. But, second, much less appreciated and rather less the focus of our attentions in this book until now, this also has major welfare implications.

The reason is very simple. Since around the turn of the century, Britain has been moving increasingly consciously from a public model of welfare to what might be seen as a 'public-plus' welfare model – residual public welfare *plus* a more individualized and privatized 'asset-based' welfare (Finlayson 2009; Hay 2013; Prabhakar 2009, 2013). The point here is that austerity has been and still is driving a further residualization of public welfare, just as the crisis has put paid to the steady asset-price appreciation on which asset-based welfare depends. It is time, one might say, to 'twist' or 'split' – not, as the governor of the Bank of England and the chancellor would seem to have conspired to do, to postpone the decision until after the general election.

To see why, we need to return to the crisis itself. As we have suggested, it was not just the Anglo-liberal growth model that was threatened by the bursting of the bubble. So too were a range of public and social policies whose development had been predicated on the assumed continuation of growth in general and of a broader asset-led conception of growth more specifically. Chief amongst these has been that very notion of asset-based welfare (Paxton 2001). This was – and remains – an approach to welfare in which citizens are encouraged to acquire, as a form of investment, appreciating assets which they might later liquidate to fund their welfare needs. It has become associated in particular with the idea that citizens, rather than the state, bear the principal responsibility for ensuring that they have (or might have) adequate funds in retirement, ill health or even unemployment to meet their needs without becoming dependent on their families (Prabhakar 2013).

In the context of an ageing population and with the projected steep decline in the per capita value of public pensions, asset-based welfare provided a means of squaring an increasingly tricky welfare circle. But the problem was that the stable and predictable asset appreciation on which it rested was, like the Anglo-liberal growth model itself, dependent on easy access to credit and the persistence of a low-inflation/low-interest rate equilibrium. It was, in other words, fine only for as long as the benign conditions of the so-called 'great moderation' persisted. These were never going to last for ever. Asset-based welfare was, in effect, a way of mortgaging the future capacity of citizens to provide for themselves with dignity on the vagaries of the housing market (and markets in other appreciating assets classes).

Put in such terms, asset-based welfare looks today like a rather risky and ultimately costly one-way accumulator bet. And it was. But, to those who assumed that the business cycle was dead, asset-based welfare was a very sensible public policy stance. For as long as asset prices were rising and there was no prospect (in the absence of a business cycle) of them falling, it was almost bound to deliver a good return to those able to participate in the process. As such, it was perfectly rational for policy-makers to promote it as a strategy for supplementing more conventional means of meeting welfare needs publicly. What made it all the more attractive to policy-makers was Britain's creeping welfare residualism from the mid-1980s (Hay and Wincott 2012). This growing residualism reinforced the incentive to promote asset-based welfare as a means of partially compensating citizens for the growing mismatch between the benefits to which they were entitled as a matter of public welfare and their expectations of the benefits they might receive.

The problem was that the attractiveness of asset-based welfare to policy-makers in Britain exceeded its capacity to deliver on a lasting basis. Indeed, despite being so widely promoted and touted, it has actually proved extremely fortunate that the transition to asset-based welfare was rather more gradual and incremental than one might have been forgiven for thinking, given the hype. In fact, by the onset of the crisis only one major asset-based welfare programme was actually up and running – the Child Trust Fund. And even this was only fully operative from 2005. Yet, despite this, close to £0.5 billion has been lost from the value of these funds since 2008. The mortgaging of childhood futures on continued asset-price appreciation has proved one of the least mourned casualties of the crisis.

Or has it? For asset-based welfare has not actually gone away; it has merely assumed a quieter form. Indeed, as hinted at above, something equivalent to asset-based welfare (a privatized alternative to public provision) looks all the more necessary in the context of pervasive welfare austerity. But, as we now know all too well, the need for asset-based welfare to compensate for a shortfall in public provision becomes all the more pressing at precisely the point when stable asset-price inflation evaporates. This is the asset-based welfare paradox which lies at the heart of Britain's current plight. And it needs to be faced up to now. The choice is a stark one: ignore the lessons of the crisis and continue to mortgage our collective futures on the bet that asset-price inflation can be made sustainable indefinitely ('twist') or share the burden of managing for our futures collectively and publicly ('split'). I guess that makes us, as proponents of a civic capitalism, 'splitters'.

And that, of course, is the point: there *is* an alternative – the civic capitalist alternative whose broad contours we have sought to set out in this book. So how do we build civic capitalism in Britain today? Or, to put it slightly differently, if civic capitalism is as we have described it, then what are the logical first steps of the transition? What needs to be done – and, above all, what needs to be done *now*?

Here, and by way of conclusion, we propose four immediate next steps – each a necessary but, in and of itself, insufficient condition of the transition towards civic capitalism in Britain.

Declaring a Commitment to Civic Capitalism

The first is, in a sense, the simplest. It is to acknowledge our plight and to commit publicly to the alternative: in short, to profess civic capitalism and to make clear its core principles. This might not seem very important. For a verbal or even a written and ostensibly binding legal commitment to civic capitalism, unless instantiated in policy, is unlikely to be worth the words with which it is spoken or the legal parchment on which it is written. But that is not quite the point. Although talk and words may indeed be cheap, we nonetheless see as imperative, as a vital prerequisite in building the kind of civic capitalism we espouse, the need for a clear, categorical and unequivocal public policy commitment to the idea that, as we have put it, capitalism must be made to serve citizens, not citizens capitalism. Only this can provide the basis of a new contract between citizens and the state and, indeed, a new role for the state – as, in effect, the gauge, custodian and guarantor of the general interest and will of the community as a whole. Such a contract also entails a new, more subservient (if not necessarily residual), place for the market – a mechanism and a device, but only one amongst many, for achieving the goals of the community as a whole. Without this new recalibration of the relationship between citizens, the state and the market, there can be no genuinely civic capitalism. For the latter requires that the state manages and regulates capitalist markets on behalf of the citizens they must be made to serve and, no less significantly, that citizens can hold the state to account (and *are provided with the means* to hold the state to account) in precisely such terms.

The implication of this is not necessarily 'more state' (in terms of the share of GDP that it consumes, for instance). But it does certainly imply a different remit for the state, a wider and more encompassing role and a much clearer and more consistent rationale for its interventions. It also entails, crucially, an end to the appeal to pure economic imperatives and logics of economic necessity or compulsion: in short, an end to governance by economic technocracy. As we have suggested, the idea that 'there is no alternative' is never the statement of an economic fact; it is always the perpetration of a political fiction. It can no longer be tolerated. The truth is that it has served (as it still serves today) to insulate from critique precisely the practices that made (and still make) Anglo-liberal capitalism ultimately unsustainable. The principles of civic capitalism imply that, if there is a good argument (however technical) for a particular policy or policy instrument setting (a hike in the bank base rate, for instance), then it needs to be made and defended publicly and in terms accessible to citizens (even where informed by highly technical considerations).

This is an important point and it has a wider implication. For what applies to the now familiar (and invariably neoliberal or market-conforming) *economic* logic of no alternative applies with no less a force to other potential sources of more benign imperatives – like those we might be tempted to associate with considerations of environmental sustainability. Sustainability may well be a core principle of civic capitalism (in the version we have set out it certainly is), but we cannot afford to substitute a civic capitalist logic of environmental compulsion for neoliberal logics of economic compulsion. Civic capitalism requires us to make and defend the case for the choice (in this case, the choice for environmental sustainability) wherever there is a choice to be made. In other words, environmental logics, just like economic logics, need to be communicated, debated and made to answer (and be seen to answer) to the public interest test that lies at the heart of a genuinely civic capitalism. In short, civic capitalist decision-making needs to be visibly deliberative, regardless of the policy domain within which it takes place.

Recalibrating the Terms of Economic Success

Declaring publicly a commitment to civic capitalism is one thing – and, as we have suggested, an important thing. But no less significant is to specify and to commit to the content of that civic capitalism more precisely. This entails both making clearer the nature of the 'civic' in civic capitalism and recalibrating our understanding of economic success in such terms. The point here is that civic capitalism can mean many things. As such, it is crucial that any incoming administration claiming civic capitalism as its animating vision is as clear as it can be about the nature of that vision – the substantive content of the civic capitalism it is offering, in other words. No less important is that it draws the link clearly and unambiguously between the civic capitalism it espouses and the measures of economic success it uses to gauge its own performance. In short, we see this recalibration of the terms of economic success as the second necessary (if, still, insufficient) condition of the transition to any form of civic capitalism.

There are a number of aspects to this, each linked to our earlier discussion of the need to change the national and, indeed, global currency of economic success. In that discussion, we suggested that civic capitalism (at least as we have defined it) should reject economic growth as the predominant global currency of economic success and thus bring to an end the fetishization of growth that has ensued (and that we see as so deeply implicated in both the global financial crisis and the more general global environmental crisis which it portends). In its place, we have made the case for a new, more complex, nuanced and compound index of economic success – the social, environmental and developmental index, or sustainable economic development index (SED). We argue now that any incoming government wedded to the kind of civic capitalism we espouse needs to be able to specify, at the point of its election (and, ideally, some time before), the constituent elements of that index (and, indeed, their relative proportion).

But this is more complicated than it might at first appear. For, as explained in our opening essay, we see the SED as itself comprised of three distinct kinds of elements: (1) those integral to the very notion of civic capitalism itself (such as measures of social inequality, environmental sustainability, health and basic welfare); (2) those which might be seen as distinctive to the variant of civic capitalism that an incoming administration might offer to the electorate (one might imagine, for instance, more or less centralized, more or less republican, possibly even more or less market-oriented variants of civic capitalism advocated by different political parties); and (3) those which, in the spirit of civic capitalism, need to be established collectively and deliberatively.

Logically, then, any new government offering a civic capitalist vision to the electorate needs to be able to answer four core questions:

1. What elements does it consider integral to a civic capitalism SED and how does it propose to gauge and measure them?
2. What, if any, additional elements does it see as distinctive to the specific variant of civic capitalism it is advocating and how does it propose to gauge and measure these?
3. What, if any, elements of the civic capitalism SED it proposes will be subject to collective public deliberation and how will such public deliberation be conducted?
4. What are the government's targets for achieving success gauged in terms of the SED (and the constitutive indices from which it is comprised) over the duration of its tenure in office (and beyond) and how will it monitor, police and even punish selective under-performance relative to such targets?

A British government setting out clearly its answer to these four questions has the credible basis, we would contend, for a civic capitalist contract with British citizens – as well as a clear and transparent set of criteria by which its performance in office might be judged.

Regulating Financial Markets for a Purpose

In addition to committing itself clearly and publicly to the core tenets of civic capitalism and to articulating, no less clearly and transparently, the content of the civic capitalist vision it is advocating (by committing itself in advance to an alternative currency of economic success and a means to gauge and measure progress with respect to its attainment), we also see as integral to any civic capitalism the adoption of a fundamentally different attitude to financial market regulation. This, too, we see as a necessary condition of the transition we advocate.

Though the point is one that we have already set out in general terms in some detail, it is important to reiterate it in the light of the specificity of the British case. For Britain has for far too long sought to make a virtue of its comparative financial market deregulation – often in the name of defending financial innovation and the contribution to British GDP thereby generated. The argument has tended to take a familiar form. Regulation precludes or, at least, crowds out and disincentivizes financial innovation, driving it offshore. Britain is good at financial innovation and hence is likely to benefit significantly from a deregulatory disposition with respect to financial markets which can only serve to reaffirm the competitive advantage it already enjoys in such markets.

As we have suggested, this is a dangerous argument and one profoundly implicated in the global financial crisis itself. For, arguably and to take merely one example, the mortgage-backed securitization so central to the bursting of the sub-prime housing bubble in the United States, which of course precipitated the crisis, could not have happened in the absence of the consistently deregulatory disposition of consecutive British governments since the 1980s. Moreover, if bank bail-outs are now reinterpreted as the price we have paid for the contribution of financial innovation to British GDP in the years before the crisis, the balance sheet (even one couched in purely monetary terms) does not look very healthy. As this suggests, whilst financial innovation may well have contributed to growth through the 'great moderation' which preceded the crisis, this is surely growth that we can live without.

This in turn suggests to us that advocates of civic capitalism need to commit publicly to the principle of discretionary precaution, as we have termed it, in economic regulation – and, indeed, not just that associated with financial markets. With respect to financial markets specifically, we argue that the implication of the transition to civic capitalism is that policy-makers and regulators should adopt a strong and overriding presupposition against all financial innovation in the absence of a strong countervailing case couched in terms of the general interest. This, too, we see as a core tenet of the sustainable development we are advocating and a necessary early step in the transition to the civic capitalism we espouse.

But financial re-regulation is not an end in itself – or, at least, not a civic capitalist end in itself. For it genuinely to promote and sustain civic capitalism in Britain, as indeed anywhere, it has to be oriented to a more collective goal. That goal we see as the reorientation of finance, at least domestically, for a more productive purpose.

Britain, as has been widely acknowledged for close to fifty years in what is now an extensive literature, has been consistently starved of investment in industrial innovation and infrastructure (see, for instance, Gamble 1994; Gerschenkron 1965; Ingham 1984; Watson and Hay 1998). This is in large part and increasingly because of the size, character and focus of its financial institutions – which make a large and growing proportion of their profits through short-selling and financial intermediation. Indeed, this too has proved tragically contagious. One of the great ironies of the financial crisis is that one of very first European banks to be bailed out was a German regional industrial bank. Chasing the lucrative returns to be had on US mortgage-backed securities and associated financial derivatives, it had increasingly abandoned its long-term focus on supplying dedicated capital to German regional industries to gorge itself instead on these shiny (and seemingly high-yielding) new financial instruments. It was, accordingly, massively exposed when the bubble burst.

What this underlines once more is that short-term speculative flows in financial markets are not only economically destabilizing; they also crowd out, in effect, investment in the real economy. That is what Britain now desperately needs – to resuscitate its industrial sector and to boost its cultural industries, to generate new investment in greener technologies and, above all, to build a new and more sustainable public infrastructure (see especially Jenkins 2013). Such a 'rebalancing' of the economy is much touted. But, as yet, there is little sense of what is entailed (Berry 2013; Berry and Hay forthcoming). From a civic capitalist perspective, it must start with the wholesale reform, re-regulation and restructuring of Britain's financial institutions – and a refocusing of the credit lines they supply from the inflation of asset-price bubbles to the long-term investment in the productive economy and the infrastructural innovation that Britain so desperately needs.

To be clear, this too has implications. Although such a vision is of course compatible with a range of substantive policies and initiatives, it can only be delivered in our view through a return to an active and, where necessary, interventionist industrial policy. This needs to be able to identify, whether nationally or at a regional level, strategically significant sectors and sub-sectors that are integral to the development of the economy – and to target the supply of both public and private investment towards them. Economies, as we know, do not transform themselves; the extent of the rebalancing required in Britain today can only be led by the state (Mazzucato 2013).

Projecting Civic Capitalism Internationally

We live in an integrated world economy – albeit, as the global financial crisis graphically reminds us, a far from perfectly integrated world economy. And that has profound implications for the argument we have made. Civic capitalism in one country, as we have sought to make clear from the outset, is not an option. This is, in part, because civic capitalism is designed as a solution to a problem or a set of problems which is global in scope and scale and, in part, because the very conditions of existence of civic capitalism domestically are, to a significant extent, international, indeed global. This means that advocates of civic capitalism on a domestic stage must also prove themselves successful advocates of civic capitalism internationally and globally. There are, in other words, a series of international/global coordination problems which British exponents of civic capitalism need to grapple with if it is to emerge as a solution to our problems either domestically or internationally.

There are many of these. But it is with four of the most immediate and obvious that we conclude.

1. It is important to think of civic capitalism as a set of principles that should apply just as much to the institutions of global governance as the apparatus of British government alone. Indeed, if this is not done, and done successfully, there is a real risk that life will be quickly squeezed out of civic capitalism in Britain by the persistence of a hostile external environment. As it happens, there presently exists a great opportunity for an incoming British government to push a civic capitalist agenda globally because work still continues internationally to define the global development framework that will succeed the United Nations Millennium Development Goals (MDGs) when they come to an end in 2015.

2. As we have said, it is only if we move away from growth as the global currency of economic success that we can begin to build a more sustainable future. As such, whilst starting to gauge economic performance domestically in more complex and sophisticated terms (using SED indices, for instance), it is important too that we coordinate regionally and globally our search for appropriate measures of economic performance which might allow us to value more highly considerations other than economic output growth alone. Ultimately, we need to be able to assign the measurement of economic success in such terms to a set of newly empowered institutions of global governance. Here an obvious candidate to be assigned this more central role of measurement and monitoring is the United Nations Development Programme (UNDP) which has for many years published a Human Development Index that meets some at least of the ambitions we set for a civic capitalist SED.

3. In the interim, it is imperative of course that the hawkish imposition of austerity does not preclude the smooth

transition, through a combination of public and private investment, to new models of economic development based on more sustainable technologies and less reliant on financial innovation and asset-appreciation dynamics. This in turn requires the international (again, ideally, global) coordination of debt and growth management as we make the transition to a new global currency of economic success. On this front, the arenas in which an incoming British government committed to a new model of capitalism would need to be active and take initiatives are obvious. They are the European Union, with which major structural reform to make the institutions of regional cooperation work more effectively for the peoples of Europe is now urgently needed, and the G20, which faces a slow drift towards irrelevance unless it is again led more actively in the spirit of balanced, energetic and fair global economic management.

4. Finally, financial market regulation – and, in particular, the adoption of the kind of discretionary precautionary principle we have called for – is much more effectively achieved globally than domestically. States like Britain, characterized by their long-standing deregulatory disposition and their relative dependence on the provision of financial services, are well placed to lead the debate – though in a sense they also have most to lose. But, since a sustainable future for Britain and the world economy alike relies on a more stable financial architecture, there can be no place for sectional national interests in questions as important as this. Britain needs to face up to its responsibilities and that may well entail some short-term sacrifice – though the possibility of negotiating access to structural funds from the IMF to ease the transition to a reduced dependence on financial services should not be discounted. Indeed, it would make a great deal of sense for Britain's government to devote top-level political attention to its engagement with the IMF, which is after all the only, and therefore the best available, agency of global financial coordination that the world possesses. The case for this is not only one of potential national

necessity: it draws as well on the present need, worldwide, for the existence of an active, sympathetic but effective agency committed to supporting the difficult shift everywhere towards the pursuit of more sustainable means of achieving collective human well-being.

These areas of action constitute a very different kind of future 'foreign policy' for Britain to that traditionally set out under this rubric. But they would unquestionably sustain the country's domestic goals in a way that has manifestly not been achieved by its other recent forays into global activism. Britain's government could still punch above its weight, as the famous phrase has it, but do so honourably and in the cause of helping to build a genuinely global and a genuinely civic capitalism.

References

Aghion, Philippe and Bolton, Patrick (1997) 'A Theory of Trickle-down Growth and Development'. *The Review of Economic Studies* 64(2): 151–72.

Albert, Michel (1993) *Capitalism versus Capitalism*. New York: Four Walls Eight Windows.

Beck, W. L., Van der Maesen, Laurent and Walker, Alan (eds) (1997) *The Social Quality of Europe*. The Hague: Kluwer Law International.

Beddoes, Zanny Minton (2012) 'For Richer, for Poorer'. *The Economist*, 13 October.

Bernanke, Ben (2011) 'Implementing a Macroprudential Approach to Supervision and Regulation'. Speech given at the *47th Annual Conference on Bank Structure and Competition*, Chicago, Illinois, May.

Berry, Craig (2013) *Are We There Yet? Growth, Rebalancing and the Pseudo-Recovery*. SPERI Paper No. 7, SPERI, University of Sheffield, UK, available at: http://speri.dept.shef.ac.uk/wp-content/uploads/2013/01/SPERI-Paper-No.7-Are-We-There-Yet-PDF-747KB.pdf

Berry, Craig and Hay, Colin (forthcoming) 'The Great British "Rebalancing" Act: The Construction and Implementation of an Economic Imperative for Exceptional Times'. *The British Journal of Politics & International Relations*.

Block, Fred (2014) 'Democratizing Finance'. *Politics & Society* 42(March): 3–28.

Blyth, Mark (2013) *Austerity: The History of a Dangerous Idea.* Oxford: Oxford University Press.

Bowman, Andrew, Froud, Julie, Joha, Sukhdev et al. (eds) (2014) *The End of the Experiment?* Manchester: CRESC.

Bush, President George W. (2008), cited in 'Talks Implode during a Day of Chaos: Fate of Bailout Plan Remains Unresolved'. *The New York Times*, 25 September.

Carney, Mark (2014) Speech delivered at the Mansion House, 12 June.

Carrington, Damien (2013) 'Global Carbon Dioxide in Atmosphere Passes Milestone Level'. *The Guardian*, 10 May.

Coates, David (2000) *Models of Capitalism.* Cambridge: Polity.

Cockett, Richard (1994) *Thinking the Unthinkable: Think-Tanks and the Economic Counter-Revolution 1931–1983.* London: Harper Collins.

Commission on the Measurement of Economic Performance and Social Progress (2009) *Final Report.* Paris, available at: www.Sen-Stiglitz-Fitoussi.fr

Conway, Ed (2014) *The Summit: The Biggest Battle of the Second World War – Fought behind Closed Doors.* London: Little, Brown.

Crouch, Colin (2004) *Post-Democracy.* Cambridge: Polity.

Crouch, Colin (2005) 'Models of Capitalism'. *New Political Economy* 10(4): 439–56.

Crouch, Colin (2008) 'Privatised Keynesianism: An Unacknowledged Policy Regime'. *The British Journal of Politics & International Relations* 11(3): 382–99.

Crouch, Colin (2011) *The Strange Non-Death of Neoliberalism.* Cambridge: Polity.

Crouch, Colin (2013) *Making Capitalism Fit for Society.* Cambridge: Polity.

Crouch, Colin (forthcoming) *Governing Social Risks in Post-Crisis Europe.* Cheltenham: Edward Elgar.

Demailly, Damien, Chancel, Lucas, Waisman, Henri and Guivarch, Celine (2013) *A Post-Growth Society for the 21st Century – Does Prosperity Have to Wait for the Return of Economic Growth?* New Prosperity. Paris: Institut du développement durable et des relations internationales, available at:

http://www.iddri.org/Publications/Collections/Analyses/Study 0813_DD%20et%20al._post-growth%20society.pdf

Eichengreen, Barry (2012) *Exorbitant Privilege*. Oxford: Oxford University Press.

Engelen, Ewald, Ismail Ertürk, Julie Froud et al. (2011) *After the Great Complacence: Financial Crisis and the Politics of Reform*. Oxford: Oxford University Press.

Finlayson, Alan (2009) 'Financialisation, Financial Literacy and Asset-based Welfare'. *British Journal of Politics & International Relations* 11(3): 400–21.

Fraser, Nancy (2014) 'Behind Marx's Hidden Abode'. *New Left Review* 86(April): 55–72.

Fukuda-Parr, Sakiko (2010) 'Reducing Inequality – The Missing MDG: A Content Review of PRSPs and Bilateral Donor Policy Statements'. *IDS Bulletin* 41(1): 26–35.

Gamble, Andrew (1994) *Britain in Decline*, 4th edn. Basingstoke: Palgrave Macmillan.

Gamble, Andrew (2014) *Crisis without End? The Unravelling of Western Prosperity*. Basingstoke: Palgrave Macmillan.

Gerschenkron, Alexander (1965) *Economic Backwardness in Historical Perspective*. Cambridge, MA: Harvard University Press.

Gough, Ian (1979) *The Political Economy of the Welfare State*. Basingstoke: Palgrave Macmillan.

Gough, Ian (2011) *Climate Change and Public Policy Futures*. London: British Academy.

Gough, Ian (2014) *Climate Change and Sustainable Wellbeing: An Argument for the Centrality of Human Needs*. CASE Paper 182. LSE, 2014.

Grubb, Michael, Hourcade, Jean-Charles and Neuhoff, Karsten (2013) *Planetary Economics: Energy, Climate Change and the Three Domains of Sustainable Development*. London: Routledge.

Haldane, Andrew G. and May, Robert M. (2011) 'Systemic Risk in Banking Ecosystems'. *Nature* 469: 351–5.

Hall, Peter A. and Soskice, David (eds) (2001) *Varieties of Capitalism*. Oxford: Oxford University Press.

Hall, Stuart, Massey, Doreen, and Rustin, Michael (2014) 'After Neoliberalism? The Kilburn Manifesto'. *Soundings* 51(3): 8–22.

Harvey, David (2010) *The Enigma of Capital and the Crises of Capitalism*. London: Profile Books.

Hay, Colin (2007) *Why We Hate Politics*. Cambridge: Polity.

Hay, Colin (2011) 'Pathology without Crisis? The Strange Demise of the Anglo-liberal Growth Model'. *Government and Opposition* 46(1): 1–31.

Hay, Colin (2013) *The Failure of Anglo-liberal Capitalism*. Basingstoke: Palgrave Macmillan.

Hay, Colin and Wincott, Daniel (2012) *The Political Economy of European Welfare Capitalism*. Basingstoke: Palgrave Macmillan.

Hemerijck, Anton (2012) *Changing Welfare States*. Oxford: Oxford University Press.

Hensarling, Jeb (2014) 'Oversight of Dodd-Frank Act Implementation', The Committee on Financial Services, House of Representatives, US Congress, Washington DC, 23 July, available at: http://financialservices.house.gov/dodd-frank/

Hirst, Paul (1994) *Associative Democracy: New Forms of Economic and Social Governance*. Cambridge: Polity.

Hoffmann, Matthew J. (2014) 'Global climate governance'. In Anthony Payne and Nicola Phillips (eds), *Handbook of the International Political Economy of Governance*. Cheltenham: Edward Elgar.

Ingham, Geoffrey (1984) *Capitalism Divided?* London: Macmillan.

Jackson, Tim (2009) *Prosperity without Growth: Economics for a Finite Planet*. London: Earthscan.

Jones, Owen (2014) *The Establishment and How They Get Away with It*. London: Allen Lane.

Jones, Richard (2013) *The UK's Investment Deficit and How to Repair It*. SPERI Paper No. 6, SPERI, University of Sheffield, UK, available at: http://speri.dept.shef.ac.uk/wp-content/uploads/2013/10/SPERI-Paper-No-6-The-UKs-Innovation-Deficit-and-How-to-Repair-it-PDF_1131KB.pdf

Kaus, Mickey (1992) *The End of Equality*. New York: Basic Books.

Kelly, Gavin (2014a) 'SeaTac: The Small US Town that Sparked a New Movement against Low Wages'. *The Observer*, 23 February, available at: http://www.theguardian.com/world/2014/feb/22/seatac-minimum-wage-increase-washington

Kelly, Gavin (2014b) 'The Self-Employed are Like Canaries in the Mine: Yet Osborne and Carney Ignore All 4.5 million of Them'. *The Guardian*, 10 July, available at: http://www.theguardian.com/commentisfree/2014/jul/10/self-employed-osborne-carney-economic-policy

Keynes, John Maynard (1933) 'National Self-Sufficiency.' *The Yale Review* 22(4): 755–69.

Keynes, John Maynard (1936) *The General Theory of Employment, Interest and Money*. London: Macmillan.

King, Anthony and Crewe, Ivor (2013) *The Blunders of Our Governments*. London: Oneworld Publications.

King, Mervyn (2013) 'Challenges for the Future'. *International Journal of Central Banking*, 9(S1): 359–65.

Klein, Naomi (2007) *The Shock Doctrine*. London: Penguin.

Konings, Martijn (2012) 'Imagined Double Movements: Progressive Thought and the Specter of Neoliberal Populism'. *Globalizations* 9(4): 609–22.

Krugman, Paul (2008) *The Return of Depression Economics and the Crisis of 2008*. London: Penguin.

Krugman, Paul (2013) *End this Depression Now!* London: Penguin.

Lakoff, George (2004) *Don't Think of an Elephant! Know Your Values and Frame the Debate*. White River Junction, VT: Chelsea Green Publishing.

Lansley, Stewart (2006) *Rich Britain: The Rise and Rise of the New Super-Wealthy*. London: Politico's.

Lansley, Stewart (2012) *The Cost of Inequality: Why Economic Equality is Essential for Recovery*. London: Gibson Square Books.

Levitas, Ruth (2005 [1998]) *The Inclusive Society? Social Exclusion and New Labour*. London: Palgrave Macmillan.

Levitas, Ruth (2013) *Utopia as Method: The Imaginary Reconstitution of Society*. London: Palgrave Macmillan.

Marquand, David (1988) *The Unprincipled Society*, new edn. London: Fontana Press.

Mazzucato, Mariana (2013) *The Entrepreneurial State: Debunking Public vs. Private Sector Myths*. London: Anthem Press.

McGinnity, Frances and Russell, Helen (2013) 'Work–Family Conflict and Economic Change', in D. Gallie (ed.), *Economic Crisis, Quality of Work and Social Integration: The European Experience*. Oxford: Oxford University Press.

Mirowski, Philip (2013) *Never Let a Serious Crisis Go to Waste*. London: Verso.

Morel, Natalie, Palier, Bruno and Palme, Joakim (2012) *Towards a Social Investment Welfare State?* Bristol: Policy Press.

Mulgan, Geoff (2010) 'Civil Society is Leading the Way on Societal Reform. Let It'. *The Guardian*. 15 March, available at:

http://www.theguardian.com/society/joepublic/2010/mar/15/civil-society-carnegie-inquiry

New Economics Foundation (2008) *A Green New Deal*. London: New Economics Foundation, available at: http://s.bsd.net/nefoundation/default/page/file/8f737ea195fe56db2f_xbm6ihwb1.pdf

Noll, Heinz-Herbert (2011) 'The Sen-Stiglitz-Fitoussi Report: Old Wine in New Skins? Views from a Social Indicators Perspective'. *Social Indicators Research* 102(1): 111–16.

Nozick, Robert (1974) *Anarchy, State and Utopia*. Oxford: Blackwell.

Obama, President Barack (2013) 'Remarks by the President on Economic Mobility'. The White House, Washington DC, 4 December, available at: http://www.whitehouse.gov/the-press-office/2013/12/04/remarks-president-economic-mobility

Oesch, Daniel (2006) *Redrawing the Class Map: Stratification and Institutions in Britain, Germany, Sweden and Switzerland*. Basingstoke: Palgrave Macmillan.

Osborne, George (2014) Speech delivered at the Mansion House, 12 June.

Ostrom, Elinor (1990) *Governing the Commons*. Cambridge: Cambridge University Press.

Oxfam (2014) *Working for the Few: Political Capture and Economic Inequality*. Oxfam Briefing Paper 178, Oxford, 20 January.

Paxton, Will (ed.) (2001) *Asset-Based Welfare: International Experiences*. London: Institute for Public Policy Research.

Payne, Anthony (2005) *The Global Politics of Unequal Development*. Basingstoke: Palgrave Macmillan.

Payne, Anthony (2013) 'Unpacking the 2013 Human Development Index'. *SPERI Comment*, 16 May, available at: http://speri.dept.shef.ac.uk/2013/05/16/unpacking-2013-human-development-index/

Pearce, Nick (2014) 'Labour Can't Spend its Way to Equality. Here's an Alternative Plan'. *The Guardian*, 18 June, available at: http://www.theguardian.com/commentisfree/2014/jun/18/labor-spend-equality-society-growth-redistribution-wealth.

Peston, Robert (2008) *Who Runs Britain?* London: Hodder.

Piketty, Thomas (2014) *Capital in the Twenty-First Century*. Cambridge, MA: Harvard University Press.

Prabhakar, Rajiv (2009) 'Asset Inequality and the Crisis'. *Renewal* 17(4): 75–80.

Prabhakar, Rajiv (2013) 'The Development of Asset-based Welfare: The Case of the Child Trust Fund in the UK'. *Policy and Politics* 37(1): 129–43.

Reed, Howard and Lawson, Neal (2011) *Plan B: A Good Economy for a Good Society*. London: Compass.

Rockström, Johan, Steffen, Will, Noone, Kevin et al. (2009) 'A Safe Operating Space for Humanity'. *Nature* 461: 472–5.

Rolf, David (2013) 'Labor: Building a New Future'. *Democracy* 29 (Summer): 42–6, available at: http://www.democracyjournal.org/pdf/29/labor_building_a_new_future.pdf

Ruggie, John G. (1982) 'International Regimes, Transactions and Change: Embedded Liberalism in the Postwar Economic Order'. *International Organization* 36(2): 379–415.

Saez, Emmanuel (2013) 'Striking it Richer: The Evolution of Top Incomes in the United States'. Paper produced at the University of California, Berkeley, 3 September, available at: http://www.elsa.berkeley.edu/~saez/saez-UStopincomes-2012.pdf

Schmidt, Vivien (2002) *The Futures of European Capitalism*. Oxford: Oxford University Press.

Schmidt, Vivien and Thatcher, Mark (eds) (2013) *Resilient Liberalism in Europe's Political Economy*. Cambridge: Cambridge University Press.

Schor, Judith (2012) *Working Hours in the Debate about Growth and Sustainability*. Paper presented to nef/CASE About Time Colloquium 12 January. London: London School of Economics and Political Science.

Seldon, Arthur (1990) *Capitalism*. Oxford: Basil Blackwell.

Sen, Amartya (1993) 'Capability and Well-being', in Martha Nussbaum and Amartya Sen (eds), *The Quality of Life*. Oxford: Clarendon Press.

Skidelsky, Robert and Skidelsky, Edward (2012) *How Much is Enough: Money and the Good Life*. London: Penguin.

Stanley, Liam (2014) ' "We're Reaping What We Sowed": Everyday Crisis Narratives and Acquiescence to the Age of Austerity'. *New Political Economy*, available at: http://www.tandfonline.com/doi/abs/10.1080/13563467.2013.861412#.VDu-qcstC70

Stiglitz, Joseph (2013) 'Inequality is Holding Back the Recovery'. *The New York Times*, 19 January.

Streeck, Wolfgang (2014a) *Buying Time: The Delayed Crisis of Democratic Capitalism*. London: Verso.

Streeck, Wolfgang (2014b) 'Ends of Capitalism'. *New Left Review* 87(May/June): 35–64.

Taylor, Matthew (2014) *Beyond Belief – Towards a New Methodology of Change.* August 24, available at: http://www.matthewtaylorsblog.com/uncategorized/beyond-belief-towards-a-new-methodology-of-change/

Unger, Roberto (1998) *Democracy Realised: The Progressive Alternative.* London: Verso.

Unger, Roberto (2007) *The Self Awakened: Pragmatism Unbound.* London: Verso.

Vandenbroucke, Frank, Hemerijck, Anton and Palier, Bruno (2011) 'The EU Needs a Social Investment Pact'. Opinion Paper 5 May 2011. Brussels: Observatoire Social Européen.

Waring, Marilyn (1989) *If Women Counted: A New Feminist Economics.* London: Macmillan.

Watson, Matthew (2010) 'House Price Keynesianism and the Contradictions of the Modern Investor Subject'. *Housing Studies* 25(3): 413–26.

Watson, Matthew (2014) *Uneconomic Economics and the Crisis of the Model World.* Basingstoke: Palgrave Macmillan.

Watson, Matthew and Hay, Colin (1998) 'In the Dedicated Pursuit of Dedicated Capital: Restoring an Indigenous Investment Ethic to British Capitalism'. *New Political Economy* 3(3): 407–26.

Wilkinson, Richard and Pickett, Kate (2009) *The Spirit Level: Why More Equal Societies Almost Always Do Better.* London: Allen Lane.

Willetts, David (1994) *Civic Conservatism.* London: Social Market Foundation.

World Economic Forum (2013) *Global Risks 2014*, available at: http://www.weforum.org/issues/global-risks

WWF (2012) *Living Planet Report 2012*, available at: http://www.wwf.org.uk/what_we_do/about.../living_planet_report_2012/

YouGov (2010) 'Financial Governance', available at: http://today.yougov.co.uk/commentaries/adele-gritten/financial-confidence

Index